THE SANCTUARY, 1844, AND THE PIONEERS

THE SANCTUARY, 1844, AND THE PIONEERS

PAUL A. GORDON

Review and Herald Publishing Association
Washington, DC 20039-0555
Hagerstown, MD 21740

This book was

Edited by Gerald Wheeler

Designed by Richard Steadham

Library of Congress Cataloging in Publication Data

Gordon, Paul A., 1930-
   The sanctuary, 1844, and the pioneers.

   Bibliography: p.
   1. Sanctuary doctrine (Seventh-day Adventists)
2. Seventh-day Adventists—Doctrines. I. Title.
BX6154.G65   1983   236'.3   83-17611
ISBN 0-8280-0217-7

About This Book

Events of the past few years have pushed the subject of the doctrine of the sanctuary and the investigative judgment into the forefront of interest and discussion as never before. Some have charged that Seventh-day Adventists did not derive it from Scripture, but from the writings of Ellen White.

Elder Paul Gordon has investigated this charge, and convincingly shows that such Adventist pioneers as J. N. Andrews, James White, and Uriah Smith based the sanctuary doctrine on a consensus reached after they had done diligent Bible study. The distinctive sanctuary doctrine does not rest on the writings of Ellen White, as some have mistakenly assumed, but is the result of a long period of careful searching and wrestling with Scripture in light of the 1844 experience. The evidence simply does not support the charge that Ellen White originated the present sanctuary doctrine.

But the author does not intend that the reader consider his book a full and complete account of how the pioneers developed and reached their consensus. Rather, Gordon takes up his study mainly at the point where they have largely come to their consensus. The author doesn't intend his book to prevent further research into how the pioneers grappled with the scriptural issues of the sanctuary and judgment. Nor does he claim that he has fully and exhaustively presented the current consensus.

The author has let the pioneers speak for themselves as far as possible. He felt that it was the fairest way of depicting what the pioneers thought and taught.

The Publisher

Contents

The Purpose of This Book

The year was 1905, and Ellen White was 77 years old. Settled in her home, Elmshaven, in California, busy preparing books, she did not know whether she wanted to cross the United States to attend the General Conference session in Washington, D.C. As the time neared, however, she wrote, "If I have to bear the burden of the perplexities here at home, and must write constantly to the brethren assembled, I feel that I would prefer to be on the field of battle rather than where it takes two weeks to write and receive a reply."—Letter 111, 1905. And so, having made the decision to go, she boarded a train in northern California for the six-day trip.

At the session, during a series of early-morning hearings before a committee of twenty-five appointed by the General Conference, a minister by the name of Albion F. Ballenger presented his new views on the sanctuary. He maintained that the holy place ministry in the sanctuary was an Old Testament experience. On May 21, Ballenger summed up his position on the sanctuary in nine theses. He then concluded that "when you allow the first apartment work to represent the plan of salvation from creation to the cross, everything is a perfect fit, and all seems beautiful and harmonious."—Partial transcript of meeting before committee of 25.

He also held that when Christ ascended to heaven after His resurrection, He went to the Most Holy Place and began His ministry there as our High Priest. Such conclusions obviously did not harmonize with the historic position of the Seventh-day Adventist Church—believed and taught from its beginning days—that Jesus entered the holy place in heaven's sanctuary at His ascension, and the Most Holy Place on October 22, 1844, to begin an

9

investigative judgment.

Ellen White did not agree either with Ballenger's methods or with his message. "The Lord has instructed me that he has misinterpreted texts of Scripture, and given them a wrong application."—Manuscript 145, 1905. Her instructor in vision, she said, wanted her to tell him, "You are bringing in confusion and perplexity by your interpretation of the Scriptures."—Manuscript 62, 1905. "I am bidden," she continued, "to say in the name of the Lord that Elder Ballenger is following a false light. The Lord has not given him the message that he is bearing regarding the sanctuary service."—Ibid.

To church leaders at the General Conference session she proclaimed, "In clear, plain language I am to say to those in attendance at this conference that Brother Ballenger has been allowing his mind to receive and believe specious error."—Ibid.

The next year, writing again of Ballenger's teaching, she said, "Brother Ballenger's position is not according to the word of God. . . . He misapplies scriptures. Theories of the kind that he has been presenting, we have had to meet again and again."—Letter 50, 1906.

Not long after the 1905 General Conference, Ballenger separated from the Seventh-day Adventist Church. But he was neither the first nor the last to disagree with the sanctuary teaching of the church. B. F. Snook and W. H. Brinkerhoff, conference officials in Iowa, broke away from the church in the middle 1860s. D. M. Canright departed in 1887. Dr. John Harvey Kellogg left at about the same time as Ballenger. L. R. Conradi, a leading European church administrator, became a Seventh Day Baptist in 1932. And we could add others to the list. All of them made the sanctuary doctrine a point of opposition. And, not surprisingly, questioning of the inspiration of Ellen White almost always accompanied their rejection, for they could not reconcile her statements with their position.

At the time of the 1905 General Conference, Ellen White gave specific advice as to how to meet Ballenger's arguments against the historic position of the Adventist Church regarding the sanctuary. "Let the aged men who were pioneers in our work speak plainly, and let those who are dead speak also, by the reprinting of their articles in our periodicals."—Manuscript 62, 1905.

In our official church publication she wrote that "we are to repeat the words of the pioneers in our work, who knew what it cost to search for the truth as for hidden treasure, and who labored to lay the foundation of our work. . . . The word given me is, Let that which these men have written in the past be reproduced."—*The*

THE PURPOSE OF THIS BOOK

Advent Review and Sabbath Herald, May 25, 1905.*

To a prominent minister she stated, "The standard-bearers who have fallen in death are to speak through the reprinting of their writings."—Letter 329, 1905.

In addition, the church should consider her writings important, as well. "The Lord would have us at this time bring in the testimony written by those who are now dead, to speak in behalf of heavenly things. The Holy Spirit has given instruction for us in these last days. We are to repeat the testimonies that God has given His people [her statements], the testimonies that present clear conceptions of the truths of the sanctuary, and that show the relation of Christ to the truths of the sanctuary so clearly brought to view."—Manuscript 75, 1905.

Ballenger's theories did not limit themselves, however, to theological differences on the sanctuary. He was involved with some aspects of the pantheistic teachings of Dr. John Harvey Kellogg, and the "holy flesh" fanaticism centering in Indiana. Both tended to emphasize immediate human perfection, here and now. Ellen White warned both Ballenger and Kellogg that their theories minimized the importance of the Sabbath, Christ's second coming, and other foundation doctrines of the church. She told them that what they taught was a modern application of the evil servant of the parable, who said, "My Lord delayeth His coming" (Manuscript 62, 1905).

That Ellen White urged reprinting of *doctrinal* presentations seems evident from her repeated reference to doctrinal errors. After quoting Jesus' warning against false prophets (Matt. 7:15-27) she said, "Let the simple doctrines of the Word shine forth in their true bearing."—*Ibid.*

Speaking at the 1905 General Conference session, she stated, "We want solid pillars for the building. Not one pin is to be removed from that which the Lord has established. The enemy will bring in false theories, such as the doctrine that there is no sanctuary."— RH, May 25, 1905.

At the same time she wrote of those "who present strange doctrines, giving the Scriptures a wrong meaning." Continuing, she said: "The doctrines that Elder Ballenger advances, if received, would unsettle our faith in the sanctuary question." Ellen White cautioned that we are not to listen to "the doctrines of men" or "doctrines that denied the truth which in the past had been

---

*Hereafter abbreviated as RH.

advocated" (Manuscript 145, 1905).

In 1906 Ellen White again spoke of those who "take texts of Scripture, and misapply them in order to make their doctrines appear as truth. The theories that Elder Ballenger advocated, which remove the sanctuary truth," she said, "are just such as the enemy would bring . . . to shake us from our foundation of faith."—Letter 40, 1906.

Mrs. White repeatedly emphasized the continuity of the sanctuary doctrine for "fifty years." One should remember this when some charge that Ellen White made substantial changes in her later years on the sanctuary doctrine. (See Manuscript Release 760, the Ellen G. White Estate.)

The purpose of this study, however, is not primarily to refute Ballenger or Kellogg, or any other attack on the sanctuary doctrine, past, present, or future. It is, rather, to let the pioneers speak. Even this purpose cannot encompass every issue or minor point. Of the many hundreds of pages of their writings to consider, we will focus on those points that seemed to come up most frequently, and that have been basic to the Adventist position.

Our examination of the pioneers will largely focus on articles that appeared in *The Present Truth* and *The Advent Review and Sabbath Herald* from 1849 to 1905, when Ellen White urged such a study. More than four hundred articles related to the subject during those years. Although we notice disagreements at times on lesser points, we also find a remarkable general unity.

Certain early writers emerge as spokesmen for the position of the church. Three stand out above all others—J. N. Andrews, James White, and Uriah Smith. They were the major presenters of our beliefs and authored almost 65 percent of the articles on the sanctuary.

Today it might seem to Adventists—and others—that the sanctuary teachings of the Seventh-day Adventist Church have largely developed from the writings of Ellen White. For many years we have had her witness easily available on the subject. But her voice was one of many on this subject, as well as on other doctrines. True, we have considered it a special voice under the direction of the Holy Spirit in visions, but it was not the only one speaking.

The author earnestly hopes that a renewed understanding of our backgrounds will strengthen faith in the divine leading of the Advent Movement. I believe you will discover that the pioneers had something to say worth considering, and that they built those conclusions on careful exposition of the Bible.

THE PURPOSE OF THIS BOOK

Because her books are readily available, this book will give references only for Ellen White's comments at the end of the major chapters. There we will also list those articles from the pioneers we have quoted. The appendix provides the larger bibliography of major articles from 1844 to 1905. Plans are being made to reproduce them in total for the student of Adventist history.

Paul A. Gordon
Ellen G. White Estate
Washington, D.C.

1

Historical Prologue

The preaching of Christ's second coming in 1844 began in such widely scattered places as England, Europe, Asia, India, Russia, Africa, South America, and the United States. Daniel 8:3-27 and 9:20-27 formed the major basis of that preaching.

James White closely tied the parable of the ten virgins, found in Matthew 25, to the expectation of Christ's return to earth. Looking back, he said, "When we take the view of this parable that has been taken by the Advent body, a harmony will be seen. The ten virgins represent those who participated, more or less, in the Advent movement. The going forth with lamps represents the movement of 1843, occasioned by the study and proclamation of the Word. 'Thy word is a lamp' (Ps. 119:105). The tarrying followed, with the slumbering time. The midnight cry in the parable represents the powerful and glorious movement, and work of God on the hearts of His people, in the autumn of 1844."—RH, April 14, 1853.

The Millerites

The Adventists—or Millerites, as they were often called in the United States because of their most prominent preacher, William Miller—were a loosely connected group. Miller himself was a Baptist, but those who followed his lead represented many churches.

At first Miller believed that the cleansing spoken of in Daniel 8:14 represented the removal of sin from the church. But continued study drew him to the conclusion that the text referred both to the cleansing of the church from sin, *and* the purification of the earth by fire at Christ's second coming. The Millerites actually experienced

15

two disappointments—the first, in the spring of 1844 without a specific date, and the second, on October 22, 1844. The latter one was the more devastating by far to those who went through it. The failure of Jesus to come as expected was a shattering experience. In confusion and uncertainty, many weeping bitterly, they asked, "Where are we now?"

Millerites Disperse

The Millerites in the United States then went in at least five directions. 1. Some abandoned any kind of religious belief altogether. 2. Others returned to their former churches. 3. Another group, quite small in number, maintained that Jesus had returned as expected, but that it had been a spiritual coming in His saints. They became known as "spiritualizers." Within ten years they had virtually disappeared. (We must not confuse them with the spiritualism of table rappings and séances.) 4. The largest segment continued to expect the imminent return of Christ. They became distinguished for "time setting," and clung to the idea that the earth was the sanctuary to be cleansed. The Advent Christian Church, today numbering some thirty thousand members, traces its roots back to them. 5. The smallest of the groups—no more than fifty to one hundred in number—strongly resisted organization for nearly twenty years. James White early called them "the scattered flock." Seventh-day Adventists have their spiritual ancestry in them. At the time of the organization of the General Conference in 1863 they still numbered only about 3,500. By 1982 they had increased a thousandfold to more than 3.5 million members around the world, with more than eighty percent outside the United States.

Seventh-day Adventist Roots

From the beginning of its life the small band that was the forerunner of the Seventh-day Adventist Church struggled with enemies committed to its destruction. Some tried to ridicule it into silence. Others determined to prove it false through what they considered to be Biblical answers to the claim for a new understanding of the cleansing of the sanctuary. Others, who had participated in Millerite preaching, simply refused to accept a new understanding of the events of 1844.

The fact that the forerunners of the Seventh-day Adventist Church believed they had someone with the prophetic gift in their ranks seemed only to fuel the fires of opposition further. Some opponents claimed that the explanations of the Disappointment and new interpretations of 1844 had come from Ellen White's visions. The historical record clearly refutes such a claim.

The Investigative Judgment and Shut Door

A new perception of the events of 1844 did not burst upon the sight of Adventists suddenly. For example, from the beginning, many believed in an understanding of a judgment *before* Christ's second coming, though it was a decade and more before the actual term "investigative judgment" appeared in Adventist publications. And though, at the beginning, there was some confusion regarding the "shut door," only a few years passed before Adventists generally agreed that the door of mercy for the world still stood open for those who had not clearly rejected the Advent message. They saw another shut door—the door of the first apartment in heaven's sanctuary—and an open one into the Most Holy Place, where Christ had entered in 1844.

The Shut Door Changes Meaning

The parable of the ten virgins formed the basis of the use of the term "shut door" at the beginning. The Millerites applied the parable to the close of probation for the world at Christ's return. For a short time *after* the 1844 disappointment many Adventists, including Ellen White, continued to hold a similar belief. But not for long. Writing in 1883, she said:

> For a time after the disappointment in 1844, I did hold, in common with the advent body, that the door of mercy was then forever closed to the world. This position was taken before my first vision was given me. It was the light given me of God that corrected our error, and enabled us to see the true position.
> I am still a believer in the shut-door theory, but not in the sense in which we at first employed the term or in which it is employed by my opponents.
> There was a shut door in Noah's day. There was at that time a withdrawal of the Spirit of God from the sinful race that perished in the waters of the Flood. God Himself gave the shut-door message to Noah:
> "My spirit shall not always strive with man, for that he also is flesh: yet his days shall be an hundred and twenty years" (Gen. 6:3).
> There was a shut door in the days of Abraham. Mercy ceased to plead with the inhabitants of Sodom, and all but Lot, with his wife and two daughters, were consumed by the fire sent down from heaven.
> There was a shut door in Christ's day. The son of God declared to the unbelieving Jews of that generation, "Your house is left unto you desolate" (Matt. 23:38).
> Looking down the stream of time to the last days, the same infinite

power proclaimed through John:

"These things saith he that is holy, he that is true, he that hath the key of David, he that openeth, and no man shutteth; and shutteth, and no man openeth" (Rev. 3:7).

I was shown in vision, and I still believe, that there was a shut door in 1844. All who saw the light of the first and second angels' messages and rejected that light, were left in darkness. And those who accepted it and received the Holy Spirit which attended the proclamation of the message from heaven, and who afterward renounced their faith and pronounced their experience a delusion, thereby rejected the Spirit of God, and it no longer pleaded with them.

Those who did not see the light, had not the guilt of its rejection. It was only the class who had despised the light from heaven that the Spirit of God could not reach.—*Selected Messages*, book 1, pp. 63, 64.

Observe that Ellen White, before a vision corrected her, believed that probation had ended for the world. Remember, she had been a Millerite who accepted such an interpretation along with others in the movement. But we find evidence that she soon changed her position. In March, 1849, Ellen White corresponded with the Hastings family, close Adventist friends. She spoke of a "Brother Stowell" who was "wavering upon the shut door." With her husband, James, she decided to visit the Stowells, and spent a week with them. The results were good. "Brother Stowell was established in the shut door and all the present truth he had doubted."—Letter 5, 1849.

What does Ellen White mean when she refers to "the shut door"? Further on in the same letter she describes a vision she had on Sabbath, March 24, just prior to visiting the Stowells.

"I saw the commandments of God and shut door could not be separated. I saw the time for the commandments of God to shine out to His people was when the door was opened in the inner apartment of the heavenly sanctuary in 1844. Then Jesus rose up and shut the door in the outer apartment and opened the door in the inner apartment and passed into the Most Holy Place, and the faith of Israel now reaches within the second vail where Jesus now stands by the ark."—*Ibid.*

The description of her vision in the letter closely parallels an account in *The Present Truth* of August, 1849, and in *Early Writings*, pages 42-45. Observe that Ellen White applied the term "shut door" not to the close of probation, but rather to the shut door of the first apartment of heaven's sanctuary.

In 1851 James White revealed a transition of understanding among the Adventist pioneers regarding the "shut door." He began by quoting Revelation 3:7:

HISTORICAL PROLOGUE

"Behold I set before thee an open door." This door Christ opens, while He shuts another. As the Philadelphia church applies to no other period than the time of the termination of the 2300 days, when Christ closed His work for the world in the Holy, and opened the door of the "Holiest of all," the conclusion seems irresistible that the open and shut door of Revelation 3:7, 8, refers to the change in the position and work of our great High Priest in the heavenly sanctuary. He then closed the work or "door" of the daily ministration in the Holy, and opened the door of the Most Holy. "*The tabernacle of the testimony*" was then opened; but before this could be done, the "door," or work of Christ's continual mediation in the Holy, had to be closed. This may well be "likened" to the shut door in the parable.

The idea that the door of God's mercy is closed or ever was to be closed to those who do not reject the offers of mercy is not found in the Bible. No such door is mentioned in Scripture. But that there ever has been a point, beyond which men may go, where, according to the plan of salvation, the intercession of Christ could not benefit them is evident.—RH, June 9, 1851.

Later White spoke of the parable of the ten virgins and the application of the term "shut door":

But what is represented by the shut door in the parable? We have shown the absurdity of applying it to the Second Advent. We can see no other application of the shut door that will harmonize with other parts of the parable, and with other scriptures, than to our High Priest entering upon the antitype of the ancient tenth day of the seventh month atonement, at the end of the 2300 days, in the autumn of 1844. His work, performing the antitype of the daily ministration, then must cease in the Holy Place of the true tabernacle, in order for him to enter the Most Holy Place to cleanse the sanctuary. And as His work closed in the Holy, it commenced in the Most Holy.—RH, April 14, 1853.

Sanctuary Foundation Beliefs

Adventist belief early established certain positions or understandings. Regarding the sanctuary, they include the following:

1. The year-day principle of prophetic interpretation applies to the seventy weeks and 2300 days of Daniel 8 and 9.

2. Daniel 8:14 speaks of the cleansing of *heaven's* sanctuary.

3. The seventy weeks and 2300 days began in 457 B.C. and the entire period ended in 1844.

4. The date, October 22, 1844, marks the moving of Christ, our High Priest, from His work in the holy place in heaven's sanctuary to the Most Holy Place.

5. The purification of the sanctuary on earth was a shadow of the cleansing of heaven's sanctuary by Christ.

6. The cleansing includes (1) an investigative judgment of all

who have claimed to accept the death of Christ as payment for their sins, (2) the applying of the merits of Christ's atonement in a final reaffirmation of the faith of the genuine believer, and (3) the blotting out of the records of pardoned sins.

7. The investigative judgment begins with the professed righteous who have already died and concludes with the avowed followers of God who are still alive. When the task is completed, probation for the world ends and Jesus prepares immediately to return to earth as King of kings.

8. The Seventh-day Adventist Church has come on the scene at the right time to preach the last message the world will receive while probation lasts.

9. The message of the first angel of Revelation 14 that "the hour of his judgment is come" is an integral part of the "everlasting gospel."

10. The sense that we are living in the time of the judgment with probation about to close gives us a special urgency as we look soberly at being found ready for Christ's return, and at the same time makes us joyful in anticipation of that great event.

Our examination will focus on the preceding aspects.

The Sanctuary Related to Other Beliefs

The pioneers among Sabbathkeeping Adventists early developed what they considered to be a system of truth. "Such is the connection, relation and dependence of one great truth upon another," Uriah Smith wrote, "that every additional evidence upon one, proportionably strengthens all the rest; and thus, by this reciprocal strength which each point furnishes to the others, the great platform of truth is established, on which God's people will finally be found standing, and which will abide the test of the great day."—RH, July 25, 1854.

Smith went on to demonstrate the connection between the Sabbath and the sanctuary. "It becomes then the duty of all those who by faith understand the work of our great High Priest in the heavenly sanctuary; who follow Him into the Most Holy, where He performs the last act of His ministration; who behold there the ark before which He ministers, and the immutable law which it contains—it becomes the duty of all such to restore the breach which has been made by Antichrist, and keep the commandments according to the requirements of God. All who believe and understand this work will do this. Thus we see that the subjects of the sanctuary and the Sabbath are inseparably connected."—*Ibid.*

More than twenty years later, he connected the sanctuary with another doctrine. This time it involved the second coming of Christ:

> The cleansing of the sanctuary leads us into a series of subjects of the most important and timely character, subjects which explain some statements of the Scriptures which are otherwise obscure, harmonize lines of prophecy otherwise disconnected, and answer some otherwise unanswerable queries which arise concerning events connected with that crowning of all events, the second coming of our Lord Jesus Christ.
>
> For instance, when Christ comes a change passes instantaneously upon the people of God, and all others are passed by. The righteous who are in their graves are raised in power, glory, and immortality, and the rest of the dead are left in their graves for a thousand years, and the righteous who are living are changed from mortality to immortality, while the rest of the living are given over to perish under the judgments of the Almighty. And this change for God's people is wrought instantaneously at the last trump. But before this change can be wrought it must be decided who are the people of God, and who are the incorrigibly wicked. This point must be decided before the Lord comes; for there is no time then for investigation and decision of character. But this work of decision is a work of judgment; and such a work of judgment must transpire before the Lord comes.—RH, Aug. 17, 1876.

Roswell F. Cottrell also recognized the close relationship of the sanctuary to the Ten Commandments, especially the Sabbath: "We find not only that the sanctuary in heaven is the grand center of the Christian system, as the earthly was of the typical, but that this subject is the center and citadel of present truth. And since our temple is in heaven, and in that temple, 'the ark of his testament,' containing 'the commandments of God,' and in the very midst of these commandments, the Sabbath of the Lord, fenced around by nine moral precepts that cannot be overthrown, it is no wonder that the enemies of the Sabbath should not only strive to abolish the ten commandments but to demolish the true sanctuary in which they are deposited beneath the mercy seat—the throne of God."—RH, Dec. 15, 1863.

Even D. M. Canright, who later left the denomination, connected the judgment in heaven's sanctuary with the doctrine of nonimmortality. "All believers in the mortality of man and the sleep of the dead agree that it is a great absurdity to teach that the righteous are taken to heaven at death, and the wicked sent to hell, and then after hundreds of years are called back, the saints from heaven, and the wicked from hell, to be judged! What can be the use of such a judgment? Is there danger that God has made a mistake in taking some to heaven who ought not to have gone there, and has sent others to hell who ought to have been in heaven? Such a judgment must be only a mockery. Hence we say, That theory must be false. God will not reward men till He has judged them to ascertain what each should have."—RH, Jan. 19, 1869.

Canright then concluded that "the fact that the saints are raised incorruptible shows that the judgment upon them is passed before they are raised."—*Ibid.*

Sunday-observing Adventists Reject a Heavenly Sanctuary

J. N. Andrews suggested that the sanctuary belief discovered by our pioneers was distasteful to some former Millerites even twenty-five years after the expected return of Christ in 1844. "Our first-day Advent brethren have never yet given this subject a candid hearing. They will not allow its discussion in their papers, nor will they listen to this in their congregations. There are, indeed, honorable exceptions; but this uncandid course is true of the greater part."—RH, April 6, 1869.

He observed that their attention, instead, focused on time setting for the second coming of Christ. "They have, however, found what they consider more worthy of their study than the Bible sanctuary. The fixing of new times for the coming of Jesus has been with many of them almost a steady source of excitement, and it has largely furnished the staple of their preaching."—*Ibid.*

By the time of Andrews' article, Seventh-day Adventists had firmly established their acceptance of the seventh-day Sabbath, and the authority of the Ten Commandments was a central belief. He explained why he believed the subject of the sanctuary might be distasteful to Sundaykeeping Adventists:

> Why are our Advent brethren so utterly averse to the study of the heavenly sanctuary? It contains within its sacred enclosure our dear, divine Redeemer. Why should it not be a precious subject of meditation to them? Shall I name the real reason? Is it not because it contains the ark of God's testament? Yet the existence of that ark in the sanctuary is the very cause of Jesus' being there to plead for us.
>
> Why should you not even look to the ark of God with intense interest? Is not the top of that ark the mercy seat? And whence is it that pardon comes to us but from the blood of sin offering there sprinkled? Guilty man cannot consent to part with the mercy seat. What then is the trouble with the ark of God? Is it not found in the fact that it contains the great original of God's law? The ark would be well enough if it were only *empty.* The mercy seat would be entirely satisfactory were it not for the objectionable thing *beneath* that mercy seat.—*Ibid.*

Andrews next developed the close connection he saw existing between the law and the sanctuary:

> And why should you object to the law of God? Is it not perfect, spiritual, holy, just, and good? In fact, if there were no law of God which condemns, there would be no occasion for a mercy seat whence pardon is obtained. If there were no law of God, there would be no atonement, no High Priest, no mercy seat, no pardon, and, in short, no sanctuary. A priest implies a sin offering; a sin offering implies guilt; guilt implies law transgressed; the law is the rule of right that reveals sin, and makes the sanctuary, the priesthood, and the atonement, necessary. It is therefore the law of God existing before the first advent of Jesus Christ that demands the atonement, and the priesthood, and the sanctuary, that sinful man may be pardoned.— *Ibid.*

Finally, he suggested the bottom line in rejecting the idea of a heavenly sanctuary:

> What fault then can you find with the moral law beneath the mercy seat? Is it not exactly this, that its fourth precept commands men to observe the Creator's rest day? And so because of the Sabbath of the Lord, men reject the law of God; and because of the law of God, they take no delight in the ark of His testament; and because of the ark, they cannot endure the idea of the heavenly sanctuary.—*Ibid.*

Conflict With Sunday-observing Adventists

The doctrinal conflict that arose between Sunday-observing Adventists and Seventh-day Adventists is a matter of historical record. We find several evidences of it, especially in the earliest articles written by our Adventist pioneers. Sunday-observing Adventists by formal resolution turned away from several doctrines: (1) The seventh-day Sabbath; (2) all spiritual gifts, including the prophetic one; and (3) a new Biblical understanding of the cleansing of the sanctuary.

By contrast, even before 1844 came to a close, those who would become pioneers in the Seventh-day Adventist Church had been introduced to, and had begun to accept, these three beliefs, which tended to unify them even without formal organization on their part.

1. The seventh-day Sabbath (Saturday). Rachel Preston, a Seventh Day Baptist, introduced the doctrine at Washington, New Hampshire, early in 1844.

2. The prophetic gift. Visions began for 17-year-old Ellen Harmon at Portland, Maine, in December, 1844, and the Portland Adventists accepted them as a genuine manifestation of the prophetic gift.

3. The two-apartment ministry of Christ in heaven's sanctuary. Hiram Edson, the morning after the Disappointment, perceived that the sanctuary to be cleansed, spoken of in Daniel 8:14, was not our earth, but the sanctuary in heaven. He also came to understand that Jesus had closed His work in the holy place, and had gone to the Most Holy Place in heaven's sanctuary to cleanse it of the sins of the righteous. Joseph Turner and Apollos Hale in the *Advent Mirror,* January, 1845, also contributed to an early understanding of the subject.

Hiram Edson's Experience

The day following the disappointment—October 23, 1844—Adventists began to have the answer to what had happened. Hiram Edson's handwritten account of his experience, though, remained unpublished and largely unknown for many years. It first appeared in print in 1921.

"Our expectations were raised high, and thus we looked for our coming Lord until the clock tolled twelve at midnight. The day had then passed, and our disappointment had become a certainty. Our fondest hopes and expectations were blasted, and such a spirit of weeping came over us as I never experienced before. It seemed that the loss of all earthly friends would have been no comparison. We wept and wept, till the day dawn. . . .

"I mused in my heart, saying: 'My advent experience has been the brightest of all my Christian experience. . . . Has the Bible proved a failure? Is there no God, no heaven, no golden city, no Paradise? Is all this but a cunningly devised fable? Is there no reality to our fondest hopes and expectations?' . . .

"I began to feel there might be light and help for us in our distress. I said to some of the brethren: 'Let us go to the barn.' We entered the granary, shut the doors about us, and bowed before the Lord. We prayed earnestly, for we felt our necessity. We continued in earnest prayer until the witness of the Spirit was given that our prayers were accepted, and that light should be given—our disappointment explained, made clear and satisfactory.

"After breakfast I said to one of my brethren, 'Let us go and see and encourage some of our brethren.' We started, and while passing through a large field, I was stopped about midway of the field. Heaven seemed open to my view, and I saw distinctly and clearly that instead of our High Priest coming out of the most holy place of the heavenly sanctuary to this earth on the tenth day of the seventh month, at the end of the 2300 days, He, for the first time, entered on that day into the second apartment of that sanctuary, and that He had a work to perform in the most holy place before coming to the earth; that He came to the marriage, or in other words, to the Ancient of Days, to receive a kingdom, dominion, and glory; and that we must wait for His return from the wedding. And my mind was directed to the tenth chapter of Revelation, where I could see the vision had spoken and did not lie. . . .

"I was closely associated with O. R. L. Crosier and Dr. F. B. Hahn, Crosier making his home with me part of the time. . . . F. B. Hahn and I were connected with Crosier in the publication of a paper called the *Day-Dawn*. Brother Hahn and I held a consultation with regard to the propriety of sending out the light on the subject of the sanctuary. We decided it was just what the remnant needed, for it would explain our disappointment and set the brethren on the right track. We agreed to share the expense between us, and said to Crosier: 'Write out the subject of the sanctuary. Get out another number of the *Day-Dawn*.' He did so, and the *Day-Dawn* was sent out bearing the light on the sanctuary subject." *—RH, June 23, 1921.

Hahn was a medical doctor; Edson, a farmer; and Crosier, a schoolteacher. We can understand why they would choose Crosier to write out the subject after several months of study together. The article in the *Day-Dawn* evidently appeared in the winter of 1845-1846. But no known copy of it exists. The *Advent Review and Sabbath Herald* of May 25, 1851, did print an excerpt from it.

A more extended article by Crosier appeared in the *Day-Star Extra*, published on February 7, 1846. In a statement written on April 21, 1847, Ellen White endorsed the later Crosier article as follows: "The Lord shew me in vision, more than one year ago, that Brother Crosier had the true light, on the cleansing of the Sanctuary, etc.; and that it was His will, that Brother C. should write out the view which he gave us in the *Day-Star Extra*, February 7, 1846. I feel fully authorized by the Lord to recommend that Extra to every saint."—*A Word to the Little Flock*, p. 12.

Early Doctrinal Study

The early Sabbathkeeping Adventists participated in concentrated doctrinal study, holding several meetings in New York and New England. James and Ellen White attended most of them. Reports of the gatherings, as found in correspondence, indicate that some of them convened to disseminate positions already arrived at, while others searched for a clearer understanding of developing doctrines. Joseph Bates in his *Vindication of the Sabbath* shows that Seventh-day Adventist beliefs were fairly well developed by as early as January, 1848. Ellen White's following description of such meetings, therefore, seems to apply more to 1847 than 1848.

"My husband, Elder Joseph Bates, Father Pierce, Elder Edson,

---

* The study by the three men confirmed Edson's convictions, but the article made no reference to the experience he had in the field on October 23. Rather it consistently appealed to scriptural authority for its conclusions.

and others who were keen, noble, and true, were among those who, after the passing of time in 1844, searched for the truth as for hidden treasure. I met with them, and we studied and prayed earnestly. Often we remained together until late at night, and sometimes through the entire night, praying for light and studying the Word."—*Selected Messages*, book 1, p. 206.

She reported that "again and again these brethren came together to study the Bible, in order that they might know its meaning, and be prepared to teach it with power."—*Ibid.*

But note still another factor:

"When they came to the point in their study where they said, 'We can do nothing more,' the Spirit of the Lord would come upon me, I would be taken off in vision, and a clear explanation of the passages we had been studying would be given me, with instruction as to how we were to labor and teach effectively. Thus light was given that helped us to understand the Scriptures in regard to Christ, His mission, and His priesthood."—*Ibid.*, pp. 206, 207.

It is obvious that even though Ellen White had seen heaven's sanctuary in several visions, she did not actively participate in all the discussions. In fact, she comments, "During this whole time I could not understand the reasoning of the brethren. My mind was locked, as it were, and I could not comprehend the meaning of the scriptures we were studying."—*Ibid.*, p. 207.

"This was one of the greatest sorrows of my life," she felt later. "I was in this condition of mind until all the principal points of our faith were made clear to our minds, in harmony with the Word of God. The brethren knew that when not in vision, I could not understand these matters, and they accepted as light direct from Heaven the revelations given."—*Ibid.*

It is important to note here that the insights on the doctrinal study given to Ellen White were *not* the basis of belief. Rather, they provided understanding of *scriptural* revelations.

The Controversy Vision of 1858

Her major vision of March 14, 1858, referred her back to the meetings of the late 1840s. "In the vision at Lovett's Grove most of the matter which I had seen ten years before concerning the great controversy of the ages between Christ and Satan, was repeated, and I was instructed to write it out."—*Life Sketches*, p. 162.

In her first written account of the 1858 vision, she vividly described the heavenly sanctuary and Christ's work there. "Jesus has risen up and shut the door of the holy place of the heavenly sanctuary and has opened a door into the most holy place and entered in to cleanse the sanctuary. . . . I was shown what did take place in heaven at the close of the prophetic periods in 1844. As Jesus ended His ministration in the holy place and closed the door of that apartment, a great darkness settled upon those who had heard and rejected the message of His coming, and they lost sight of Him."—*Early Writings,* pp. 250, 251.

Ellen White then portrayed the sanctuary in heaven as she saw it in vision. She walked through it and observed furniture like that in the sanctuary on earth. "I was also shown a sanctuary upon the earth containing two apartments. It resembled the one in heaven, and I was told that it was a figure of the heavenly."—*Ibid.,* pp. 252, 253.

She concluded with the observation that "as the priest entered the most holy once a year to cleanse the earthly sanctuary, so Jesus entered the most holy of the heavenly, at the end of the 2300 days of Daniel 8, in 1844, to make a final atonement for all who could be benefited by His mediation, and thus to cleanse the sanctuary."—*Ibid.,* p. 253.

As the Whites returned to Battle Creek from Lovett's Grove, Ohio, they stopped at the home of Adventist friends in Jackson, Michigan. There Ellen White suffered a paralyzing stroke. After prayer, she recovered enough to finish the trip home.

Painfully at first, but steadily, she produced an account of the vision. When she finished, she had a small book of 219 pages, her first *Great Controversy.* She then had another vision, which revealed the reason for her stroke. Satan had tried to kill her so she could not write out the controversy story.

The Sanctuary—A Frequent Subject for Visions

It seems that the sanctuary was a frequent subject of early visions. W. C. White, Ellen White's son, said that "regarding some features of the revelation, such as the features of prophetic chronology, as regards the ministration in the sanctuary and the changes that took place in 1844, the matter was presented to her many times and in detail many times, and this enabled her to speak very clearly and very positively regarding the foundation pillars of our faith."—Quoted in *Selected Messages,* book 3, p. 462.

The record surely agrees with his observation. We can identify at least eleven such visions between 1844 and 1851 alone:

1. February, 1845, in eastern Maine. At its beginning she saw

both the Father and Jesus sitting on a throne. Then both went into the Most Holy Place at the end of the 2300 days. See *Early Writings*, pp. 54-66, and the *Day-Star*, March 14, 1846.

2. October, 1845, location unknown. It portrayed the closing of Christ's work in the Most Holy with events in heaven and on earth. See *Ellen G. White and Her Critics*, pp. 626, 627; the *Day-Star*, March 14, 1846, and *A Word to the Little Flock*, p. 22.

3. Sometime between February and April, 1846, location unknown. She then endorsed the Crosier article on the sanctuary in the *Day-Star Extra*, February 7, 1846. See *A Word to the Little Flock*, p. 12.

4. March 6, 1846, at Fairhaven, Massachusetts. It was the first vision in which she saw the halo of light surrounding the fourth commandment in the Most Holy Place in heaven's sanctuary. See *Life Sketches*, pp. 95, 96, and *A Word to the Little Flock*, p. 21.

5. Sabbath, April 3, 1847, at Topsham, Maine. The vision took her both to the holy and Most Holy places in heaven's sanctuary. Also it confirmed the Sabbath doctrine. She wrote about it in a letter to Joseph Bates. See *Early Writings*, pp. 32-35, and *Life Sketches*, p. 100.

6. 1847-1848. It is not certain whether she had one or several visions as she and James White attended meetings in New York and New England to study our doctrines from the Bible. At the time of her 1858 great controversy vision she referred to this time when she had been shown details on many of our doctrines, including the sanctuary one. See *Life Sketches*, p. 162.

7. Sabbath, January 5, 1849, at Rocky Hill, Connecticut. She witnessed the sealing of God's people and Jesus still interceding in the Most Holy Place in heaven. See *Early Writings*, pp. 36, 37.

8. Sabbath, January 5, 1849, the same day as the previous vision. Given in connection with a healing, it portrayed Jesus clothed in priest's robes. See *Early Writings*, pp. 36-38.

9. Sabbath, March 24, 1849, at Topsham, Maine. The vision showed the shut door of the first apartment of heaven's sanctuary. See *Early Writings*, pp. 42, 43, 86, and *The Present Truth*, August, 1849.

10. September, 1850, at Sutton, Vermont. It revealed the plagues falling after the finish of the cleansing of heaven's sanctuary. See *Early Writings*, pp. 52, 53.

11. May 14, 1851, location unknown. Ellen White saw Christ's closing ministry in heaven. See *Early Writings*, pp. 70, 71.

The Vision of March 24, 1849

As an example of how Ellen White presented the sanctuary, we note a brief excerpt from her account of one early vision:

> Sabbath, March 24th, 1849, we had a sweet, and very interesting, meeting with the brethren at Topsham, Maine. The Holy Ghost was poured out upon us, and I was taken off in the Spirit to the City of the living God. There I was shown that the commandments of God, and the testimony of Jesus Christ, relating to the shut door, could not be separated, and that the time for the commandments of God to shine out, with all their importance, and for God's people to be tried on the Sabbath truth, was when the door was opened in the Most Holy Place of the heavenly sanctuary, where the ark is, containing the Ten Commandments. This door was not opened until the mediation of Jesus was finished in the Holy Place of the sanctuary in 1844. Then, Jesus rose up, and shut the door in the Holy Place, and opened the door in the Most Holy Place, and passed within the second vail, where He now stands by the ark; and where the faith of Israel now reaches.
>
> I saw that Jesus had shut the door in the Holy Place, and no man can open it; and that He had opened the door in the Most Holy, and no man can shut it (see Rev. 3:7, 8); and that since Jesus has opened the door in the Most Holy Place, which contains the ark, the commandments have been shining out to God's people, and they are being tested on the Sabbath question.
>
> I saw that the present test on the Sabbath could not come until the mediation of Jesus in the Holy Place was finished, and He had passed within the second vail; therefore, Christians who fell asleep before the door was opened in the Most Holy, when the midnight cry was finished, at the seventh month, 1844; and had not kept the true Sabbath, now rest in hope; for they had not the light, and the test on the Sabbath, which we now have, since that door was opened. . . .
>
> I saw that the enemies of the present truth have been trying to open the door of the Holy Place, that Jesus has shut; and to close the door of the Most Holy Place, which He opened in 1844, where the ark is, containing the two tables of stone, on which are written the Ten Commandments, by the finger of Jehovah.—*The Present Truth*, August, 1849.

Bible Study and Visions

Though Ellen White received confirming visions at the time of the doctrinal discussion and following, as well as those we have just noted, Adventists consistently made their final appeal to Scripture. Writing in 1874, Uriah Smith responded to a charge by a Sunday-observing Adventist, Miles Grant, who said, " 'It is claimed by the Seventh-day Adventists that the sanctuary to be cleansed at the end of the 2300 days, mentioned in Daniel 8:13, 14, is in *heaven*, and that the cleansing began in the autumn of A.D. 1844. If anyone should ask why they thus believe, the answer would be, the information came through one of Mrs. E. G. White's visions.' "—RH, Dec. 22, 1874, quoted from the *World's Crisis*, Nov. 25, 1874.

THE SANCTUARY, 1844, AND THE PIONEERS

Uriah Smith replied that "works upon the sanctuary are among our standard publications. Hundreds of articles have been written upon the subject. But in no one of these are the visions referred to as any authority on this subject, or the source from whence any view we hold has been derived. Nor does any preacher ever refer to them on this question. The appeal is invariably to the Bible, where there is abundant evidence for the views we hold on this subject."—*Ibid.*

A search of the many articles in the *Review and Herald* supports his statement. They never quote Ellen White as the authority for the sanctuary teaching of the church. In only a few instances around the turn of the century do authors mention her in reference to this, and then only incidentally.

And so we turn to the witness of the pioneers to the doctrine that is unique to the Seventh-day Adventist Church—the cleansing of the heavenly sanctuary and investigative judgment by Christ as He prepares to return to earth as King of kings.

* * * *

ARTICLES QUOTED IN THIS CHAPTER

James White
 June 9, 1851, The Parable, Matthew 25:1-12
 April 14, 1853, The Shut Door
J. N. Andrews
 April 6, 1869, The Opening of the Temple in Heaven
Uriah Smith
 July 25, 1854, The Relation Which the Sabbath Sustains to Other Points of Present Truth
 Dec. 22, 1874, The Sanctuary
 Aug. 17, 1876, The Sanctuary
Roswell F. Cottrell
 Dec. 15, 1863, The Sanctuary
D. M. Canright
 Jan. 19, 1869, The Two Absurdities
Ellen G. White
 August, 1849, Dear Brethren and Sisters *(The Present Truth)*
Hiram Edson
 June 23, 1921, The Spirit of 1844 (H. M. Kelley, quoting Edson)

2

What Is the Sanctuary?

Millerites had identified the sanctuary of Daniel 8:14 with the earth and had expected a "cleansing" of it by fire at the second coming of Christ in 1844. But when He did not return, they began almost immediately to explore several alternatives.

Crosier's *Day-Star* Article

Edson, Hahn, and Crosier, as noted earlier, were among the first to offer a new identification of the sanctuary mentioned in Daniel 8:14. Crosier wrote in the *Day-Star Extra*, February 7, 1846, that "the Sanctuary of the new covenant is not on earth, but in heaven. . . . The Sanctuary of the new covenant is connected with New Jerusalem, like the Sanctuary of the first covenant was with Old Jerusalem."

Speaking of Hebrews 9:8, Crosier said: "The Holies (two) verse 8, the way of which was not made manifest till the time of reformation, when Christ shed His own blood, belong to His 'greater and more perfect tabernacle' spoken of in the next verse."—*Ibid.*

"[Hebrews] 6:19, 20," he continued, "is supposed to prove that Christ entered the Holy of Holies at His ascension, because Paul said He had entered within the vail. But the vail which divides between the Holy and the Holy of Holies is 'the second vail,' Ch. 9:3; hence there are two vails, and that in Ch. 6, being the first of which he speaks, must be the *first* vail, which hung before the Holy, and in Ex. was called a curtain."—*Ibid.*

We can see from these brief excerpts that his position directly contradicted the Millerite one. Particularly notice three points: (1) The sanctuary is in heaven, and not on earth, (2) heaven's sanctuary has two apartments, not one, and (3) at His ascension Christ began

31

His ministration in the holy place, not the Most Holy.

Crosier, though he wrote out the conclusions of the three men, did not long remain with the Adventists, so we cannot consider him a Seventh-day Adventist pioneer. By 1853 he opposed the position of his earlier article. But James White, in commenting on an exchange of views in an Adventist publication, observed that "the *Harbinger* of March 5th has some inquiries relating to the Sanctuary by J. B. Frisbie, and answers by O. R. L. Crosier. 'My views,' says C, 'have been somewhat changed on the subject of the "sanctuary" since 1845, when I wrote the article on the law of Moses, from which Sabbatarian Adventists quote so often.' We have quoted from C's article, for no other reason than this, it contained precious truth—which we wished to spread before the flock of Christ. And God has blessed it to the good of many. One man backsliding from the truth does not affect that truth, any more than to renounce the religion of Christ destroys Christianity."—RH, March 17, 1853.

The Seventh-day Adventist Church did not accept all of Crosier's conclusions in every detail, as its early leaders more fully developed the doctrine through Bible study. But it was an important beginning.

A Literal Sanctuary

An important discussion point almost from the first was the question of a literal sanctuary in heaven. Early Seventh-day Adventists generally agreed that there was such a sanctuary. Each of them offered reasons for such a conclusion. For example, in 1851 James White said:

> We not only believe in a literal Jesus, who is a "Minister of the Sanctuary," but we also believe that the Sanctuary is literal. And more, when John says that he saw "one like the Son of man" in the midst of the seven candlesticks," that is, in the Holy Place, we know not how to make the candlesticks spiritual, and the Son of man literal. We therefore believe that both are literal, and that John saw Jesus while a "Minister" in the Holy Place. John also had a view of another part of the Sanctuary, which view applies to the time of the sounding of the seventh angel. He says, "The temple of God was opened in heaven, and there was seen in His temple the ARK OF HIS TESTAMENT." Rev. 11:19. Also, *"The tabernacle of the testimony was opened in heaven."* Chap. 15, verse 5. This being an event to take place under the sounding of the seventh angel, it could be fulfilled at no other time than at the end of the 2300 days.
>
> The Most Holy, containing the Ark of the ten commandments, was then opened for our Great High Priest to enter to make atonement for the cleansing of the Sanctuary. If we take the liberty to say there is not

a literal Ark, containing the ten commandments in heaven, we may go only a step further and deny the literal City, and the literal Son of God.—RH, June 9, 1851.

Contrary to what some might imagine, the pioneers rejoiced that Christ had begun a final judgment. A few months later, White spoke of the joy that came to the hearts of discouraged Adventists when they discovered that Jesus was interceding in a literal sanctuary in heaven for them.

"Many of the dear Advent brethren have felt much like the followers of Jesus who said, 'They have taken away the Lord,' 'and we know not where they have laid him.' But the present truth has found Him, to the joy of their hearts. We have witnessed the flowing tears of some such, as the literal Sanctuary in heaven has been pointed out, and the literal Jesus shown to be standing before the mercy seat (that is over the Ark of the Ten Commandments) still pleading His blood for the errors of His people. And we have heard them express great joy that they had found Jesus. In a number of such cases where prayer had been nearly or entirely dispensed with for four or five years, now the family altar is erected and the whole family join in vocal prayer."—RH, Feb. 17, 1852.

J. N. Andrews, writing the next year, also supported a literal sanctuary in heaven:

1. The Bible many times names the tabernacle, temple, or sanctuary, in heaven; we therefore believe that such a building exists. Heb. 8:1, 2; Ps. 102; 19; Jer. 17:12; Ps. 11:4; Isa. 6:1-6; Rev. 15:5-8; 2 Sam. 22:7; Ps. 18:6; Rev. 7:15; 11:19; 13:6; 14:15, 17; 16:1, 17; Heb. 9:11.

2. The Bible repeatedly testifies that the earthly sanctuary which consisted of two holy places [Ex. 26:33; Heb. 9:1-5] was made by Moses in strict accordance with the pattern showed to him in the mount [Ex. 25:8, 9, 40; 26:30-33; Acts 7:44]; which pattern was a representation of the heavenly sanctuary itself. Heb. 8:1-5; 9:23. We therefore believe that the heavenly tabernacle consists of holy places also; and to this agrees the fact that the word rendered "Sanctuary" in Heb. 8:3, and "holiest of all" in Chap. 9:8; 10:19, is plural, literally signifying holy places.

3. The Bible testifies that the holy places made with hands are "the figures of the true," in the greater and more perfect tabernacle. Hebrews 9:11, 12, 23, 24. We therefore feel compelled to reject the view that the two apartments of the Jewish tabernacle were the figures of two dispensations, and believe that they represent corresponding holy places in the true tabernacle.—RH, Aug. 28, 1853.

Apparently, some in 1853 believed, like Ballenger in 1905, that the holy place ministry occurred in Old Testament times, and Christ's Most Holy Place ministry began when He returned to heaven. Roswell F. Cottrell spoke of a conversation with a friend over the question of a sanctuary in heaven. The latter felt that Adventists were too literal about it. Writing with a touch of sarcasm, perhaps, Cottrell said:

> My friend thought it not necessary to understand this subject so literally, as if there was in reality a Sanctuary in the heavens. Perhaps he may discover, upon examination, that Paul ran as deep into this error as any one at the present time. "We have such an high priest," says he. What! a literal high priest? Yes, the man Christ Jesus, who ascended to heaven bodily in the sight of His disciples.
>
> Well, of course we admit that we have a literal High Priest, but we are not to understand that He ministers in a literal sanctuary.
>
> What kind of a Sanctuary, then?
>
> O, it is a figurative or spiritual Sanctuary.
>
> What is that? If I have the right idea of such a Sanctuary, it is composed of nothing.
>
> That is it; and anyone can see that it is impossible for nothing to have two apartments.
>
> We will try to understand it so. On earth there was a real, literal sanctuary pitched by man, where the priests performed their service. But Christ is "a minister of the Sanctuary and of the true tabernacle, which the Lord pitched, and not man." This Sanctuary is composed of nothing, and of course its locality is nowhere. But the Lord pitched it, and has provided a literal High Priest, having flesh and bones, to minister in it. The priests on earth served "unto the example and shadow of heavenly things." That is, they shadowed forth, by their services in the two apartments of the "worldly sanctuary," what Christ would do for His people in the heavenly, which has no existence. This is shadowy enough! A shadow of something that is less than a shadow. Then, Moses was shown nothing, or the figure of nothing, while he was on the holy mount, and was strictly charged to make every thing pertaining to the tabernacle just like it.
>
> But enough of this. Enough has been said to show the folly of spiritualizing into nothing the things in the heavens.—RH, July 24, 1855.

Uriah Smith also advocated a literal sanctuary in heaven. After quoting Hebrews 9:23, 24, he observed that the tabernacle and its sacred vessels were "patterns of things in the heavens." He went on to declare, "What! perhaps some are ready to exclaim, Do you believe that there are literal things in heaven, that there is a real Sanctuary there? Just as much as we believe that a real one ever existed on this earth. Just as literal and real as we believe the antitype of the offerings connected with the Sanctuary to be, namely Jesus, who offered Himself the great Sacrifice for the world on Calvary—so literal and real do we believe the antitype of the Sanctuary itself to be."—RH, Feb. 18, 1858.

WHAT IS THE SANCTUARY?

Smith offered Biblical support from both Old and New Testaments for a literal sanctuary in heaven. "Rev. 11:19. 'And the *temple* of God was opened *in heaven*, and there was seen in his temple the ark of his testament.' Rev. 14:17. 'And another angel came out of the *temple which is in heaven.*' Rev. 15:5. 'And after that I looked and behold the *temple* of the tabernacle of the testimony *in heaven* was opened.' Rev. 16:17. 'And the seventh angel poured out his vial into the air; and there came a great voice out of the *temple of heaven* from the throne, saying, It is done.' Ps. 11:4. 'The Lord is in his holy temple: the Lord's throne is in heaven.' Heb. 9:11, 12. 'But Christ being come an High Priest of good things to come, by a greater and more perfect tabernacle, not made with hands, that is to say, not of this building; neither by the blood of goats and calves, but by his own blood, he entered in once into the holy place having obtained eternal redemption for us.' "—*Ibid.*

He then listed several additional texts in support of a literal sanctuary in heaven. "This heavenly Sanctuary is called by Jesus 'my Father's house;' [John 14:2]; by David, Habakkuk, and John, 'the temple of God in heaven' [Ps. 11:4; Hab. 2:20; Rev. 11:19]; God's 'holy habitation' [Zech. 2:13; Jer. 25:30; Rev. 16:17]. See also Ps. 102:19; Jer. 17:12; 2 Sam. 22:7; Ps. 18:6; Isa. 6:1-6; Rev. 7:15; 13:6; 14:15, 17; 16:1, 7."—*Ibid.*

The Old Testament Sanctuary

Perhaps we should give here a summary description that Uriah Smith made of the Old Testament sanctuary on the basis of Exodus 25-31:

> It was a structure of extraordinary magnificence formed of upright boards overlaid with gold, thirty cubits long, about ten in width, and ten in height. At the east end, which was the entrance, there were five pillars of shittim wood, whose chapiters and fillets were overlaid with gold, having hooks of gold, standing on five sockets of brass. Over the tabernacle thus erected were thrown four different coverings. The first and inner curtain was composed of fine linen embroidered with figures of cherubim, in blue, purple and scarlet. This formed the magnificent ceiling. The second covering was made of goats' hair; the third of rams' skin dyed red; and the fourth and last, of badgers' skins. The east end was enclosed with a richly embroidered curtain, suspended from the pillars before mentioned.
>
> The sacred tent was divided into two apartments by means of a vail suspended from four pillars of shittim wood overlaid with gold, set in sockets of silver. In what proportion the Sanctuary was thus divided we are not informed, but it is supposed to be the same as was afterwards observed in the temple. 1 Kings 6.

In the first apartment, or holy place, were three things worthy of notice: the golden candlestick, the table of shewbread, and the altar of incense. In the second apartment or most holy place, were also three things to claim attention: the ark, the mercy seat, and cherubim. It was above the ark, over the mercy seat, between the cherubim, that God manifested His presence, and from whence He communicated with His people. Ex. 25:22. And so David prays, "Thou that dwellest between the cherubims, shine forth." Ps. 80:1.

It is to be observed that neither the holy nor the most holy place had any window; hence in the first apartment there was need of the candlestick with its seven lamps; and in regard to the second where God dwelt, Solomon said, "The Lord said that he would dwell in the thick darkness." 1 Kings 8:12.

Before the door of the tabernacle was placed the brazen laver, and the altar of burnt offering, and around the whole was erected the court with its curtains of fine twined linen.—RH, Feb. 11, 1858.

The Sanctuary in Heaven

William Miller and most of those who accepted his preaching of Christ's second coming, as we have already mentioned, accepted the generally believed idea of their day that the sanctuary was the earth or a portion of it. It led them to equate the "cleansing" of the sanctuary with the purification of the earth by fire at Christ's return. After 1844 the pioneers realized for the first time that the sanctuary was in heaven and that it had served as the pattern for the one built by Moses in the wilderness. Andrews spoke of the two sanctuaries and their history.

The sanctuary of the Bible is the habitation of Jehovah. It includes, first, the tabernacle pitched by man, which was the pattern of the true; and second, the true tabernacle, which the Lord pitched and not man. The tabernacle erected by man, as the pattern of the true, embraced, first, the tabernacle of Moses, second, the temple of Solomon, and, third, the temple of Zerubbabel. The true tabernacle of God is the great original of which Moses, Solomon and Zerubbabel erected "figures," "patterns" or "images."

We trace the pattern of the true from the time it was erected by Moses, until it was merged in the larger and more glorious pattern which Solomon caused to be established. We trace this building down to the period when it was overthrown by Nebuchadnezzar, and suffered to remain in ruins through the Babylonish captivity. And from the time that Zerubbabel rebuilt the sanctuary, we trace the history of the pattern until we reach the true tabernacle, the great sanctuary of Jehovah. We trace the history of the tabernacle from the time that our Lord entered it to minister in "the holy places" for us, forward to the time when it shall be located on the New Earth, when the tabernacle and sanctuary of God shall be with His people for ever.—RH, Jan. 6, 1853.

WHAT IS THE SANCTUARY?

James White joined his testimony with Andrews in identifying the sanctuary of Daniel 8. While serving as editor of the *Review*, he commented:

> It has been supposed that the earth, or a portion of it, was the Sanctuary of Daniel 8. This is an error that has stood in the way of the reception of the "present truth," and out of which has grown the recent fanaticisms on the definite time of the Second Advent. The definition of the word sanctuary, is a "sacred place," a "dwelling place of the Most High." This earth, or any portion of it, has not been such a place since man left Eden 6,000 years since.
>
> As the typical sanctuary of the Jews was the center of their religious system, so the "greater and more perfect Tabernacle" above, of which Jesus Christ is a High Priest, forms the center of all gospel truth. There is God the Father, there is Jesus Christ, a merciful High Priest, and there is the mercy seat, the ark, the law of God [Rev. 11:19], and the holy angels. We are indeed introducing a glorious theme. It would be far better for the spiritual interests of the people of God if they would more constantly look upward, and by faith view the glories of the heavenly Sanctuary. We recommend the reading of the book of Hebrews as an excellent commentary on this subject.—RH, Dec. 5, 1854.

Two Bible Sanctuaries

Some years later White compared and contrasted the two sanctuaries of the Bible. Noting Bible support for each point, he spoke especially of the transition from one to the other at the death of Christ on the cross:

> 1. The sanctuary of the first covenant ends with that covenant, and does not constitute the sanctuary of the new covenant. Heb. 9:1, 2, 8, 9; Acts 7:48, 49.
>
> 2. That sanctuary was a figure for the time then present, or for that dispensation. Heb. 9:9. That is, God did not, during the typical dispensation, lay open the true tabernacle; but gave to the people a figure or pattern of it.
>
> 3. When the work of the first tabernacle was accomplished, the way of the temple of God in Heaven was laid open. Heb. 9:8; Ps. 11:4; Jer. 17;12.
>
> 4. The typical sanctuary and the carnal ordinances connected with it were to last only till the time of reformation. And when that time arrived, Christ came, an high priest of good things to come by a greater and more perfect tabernacle. Heb. 9:9-12.
>
> 5. The rending of the vail of the earthly sanctuary at the death of our Saviour evinced that its services were finished. Matt. 27:50, 51; Mark 15:88; Luke 23:45.
>
> 6. Christ solemnly declared that it was left desolate. Matt. 23:37, 38; Luke 13:34, 35.
>
> 7. The sanctuary is connected with the host. Dan. 8:13. And the host, which is the true church, has had neither sanctuary nor

priesthood in old Jerusalem the past 1800 years, but has had both in Heaven. Heb. 8:1-6.

8. While the typical sanctuary was standing, it was evidence that the way into the true sanctuary was not laid open. But when its services were abolished, the tabernacle in Heaven, of which it was a figure, took its place. Heb. 10:1-9; 9:6-12.

9. The holy places made with hands, the figures or patterns of things in the Heavens, have been superseded by the heavenly holy places themselves. Heb. 9:23, 24.

10. The sanctuary since the commencement of Christ's priest-hood is the true tabernacle of God in Heaven. This is plainly stated in Heb. 8:1-6. These points are conclusive evidence that the worldly sanctuary of the first covenant has given place to the heavenly sanctuary of the new covenant. The typical sanctuary is forsaken, and the priesthood is transferred to the true tabernacle.—RH, March 1, 1870.

The Sanctuary and Sunday-observing Adventists

Sunday-observing Adventists continued to believe that the sanctuary is the earth long after 1844. Writing in 1855, Uriah Smith stated that they considered it taken "for granted" that "the 'sanctuary' is the earth" (World's Crisis, Dec. 30, 1854). Then he examined the idea:

What are some of the reasons why we should take this for granted?

1st. If the earth was the Sanctuary it would be recognized as such by the Word of God; but instead of this, it is nowhere in that Word thus recognized.

2d. If it was the Sanctuary, we should expect to find the term many times applied to it, pointing it out as such; but the fact is, the term is distinctly applied to another definite object which God calls His Sanctuary.

3d. The term sanctuary is defined, A holy place, A sacred place, A dwelling place of the Most High. Ex. 25:8. Is the earth a holy or a sacred place? "Cursed is the ground for thy sake." Gen. 3:17. Is it the habitation of God? "Thus saith the Lord, the heaven is my throne, the earth is my footstool." Isa. 66:1. "The Lord shall roar from on high and utter his voice from his holy habitation." Jer. 25:30. "For he hath looked down from the height of his sanctuary; from heaven did the Lord behold the earth." Ps. 102:19.

4th. Paul thus discourses upon the Sanctuaries of the first and second covenants: "Then verily the first covenant had also ordi-nances of divine service, and a worldly sanctuary. For there was a tabernacle made; the first wherein was the candlestick, and the table of shewbread; which is called the sanctuary [or holy, margin]; and after the second vail the tabernacle, which is called the Holiest of all," etc. Heb. 9:1-3. This refers to the building erected by Moses, at the express command of God, and in exact accordance with the pattern shown him on the mount. Ex. 25, and onward. This Paul plainly declares was the sanctuary of the first covenant.—RH, Jan. 9, 1855.

Smith next turned his attention to another sanctuary:

> With this sanctuary of the first covenant, Paul introduces another, the Sanctuary of the new covenant. He calls it a greater and more perfect tabernacle not made with hands; "the true tabernacle which the Lord pitched and not man"; "things in the heavens." The first-covenant sanctuary was a "figure for the time then present," or a pattern of the true tabernacle which should take its place when the new covenant should be established. In it "were offered both gifts and sacrifices that could not make him that did the service perfect as pertaining to the conscience; which stood only in meats and drinks, and divers washings and carnal ordinances imposed on them until the time of reformation."
>
> But the time of reformation came—Christ came an high priest of good things to come, the way of the heavenly holy places was laid open, and the earthly sanctuary gave place—not to the earth! but to the greater and more perfect tabernacle which the Lord pitched and not man, where Christ our great High Priest has entered, not with the blood of goats and calves, but by His own blood, now to appear in the presence of God for us. Heb. 8, 9.—*Ibid.*

He summed up the question by concluding that "here the sanctuaries of the two covenants are plainly set before us: the earthly pitched by man; the heavenly pitched not by man: the earthly, with its mortal priesthood, and its sacrifices of goats and calves; the heavenly with its more excellent ministry, its better mediator, and to be cleansed at last with better sacrifices. Heb. 9:23."—*Ibid.*

Can the Heavenly Sanctuary Be "Trodden Under Foot"?

Those who did not accept the idea of a sanctuary in heaven raised the objection that heaven's sanctuary, if there was one, could not be "trodden under foot" as pictured in Daniel 8:13. Uriah Smith answered them.

> It is said that if there is a sanctuary in Heaven, it cannot be the sanctuary of Dan. 8:14; for that is a sanctuary which is trodden under foot; but a sanctuary in Heaven cannot be trodden under foot.
>
> This objection is surely uttered without thought. Where is Christ? In Heaven. Can He while there be trodden under foot? If so, the sanctuary where He ministers can also be trodden under foot. And Paul says emphatically that Christ is trodden under foot by a certain class of sinners, crucified afresh, and put to an open shame. Heb. 10:29. "Of how much sorer punishment, suppose ye, shall he be thought worthy, who hath *trodden under foot the Son of God.*" How do they do this? Simply by becoming apostate and counting His blood an unholy thing, and doing despite to the spirit of grace. And how do

they tread under foot the sanctuary? By erecting rival sanctuaries, and turning mankind away from the true.—RH, June 22, 1876.

Then Smith followed with a brief listing of several false sanctuaries:

> In the days of the Judges and of Samuel, Satan's rival sanctuary was the temple of Dagon, where the Philistines worshiped. Judges 16:23, 24. After Solomon had erected a glorious sanctuary upon Mount Moriah, Jeroboam, who made Israel to sin, erected a rival sanctuary at Bethel, and thus drew away ten of the twelve tribes from the worship of the living God, to that of the golden calves. 1 Kings 12:26-33; Amos 7:13, margin. In the days of Nebuchadnezzar, the rival of the sanctuary of God was the temple of old Belus in Babylon. At a later period, there was the Pantheon or temple of "all the gods" at Rome, which, after the typical sanctuary had given place to the true, was baptized and called Christian. Thenceforward Satan had at Rome a "temple of God," in which was a being "exalted above all that is called God or that is worshipped," the man of sin, the son of perdition. And of this papal abomination it was expressly predicted that it should make war upon the saints, or tread under foot "the host," and make war upon the tabernacle of God in Heaven, or tread under foot the sanctuary above. Rev. 13:6—*Ibid.*

The Sanctuary and Other Truths

The pioneers visualized the sanctuary doctrine as a pillar connected with others to form a temple of truth. In the historical prologue we observed that they connected it with such doctrines as the Sabbath, the state of the dead, and the second coming of Christ. Uriah Smith in 1881 spoke of how a correct understanding of the sanctuary would greatly simplify other questions.

> The view that the sanctuary of the new covenant is in Heaven; that it is cleansed by the service of our great High Priest in the putting away of sins; that this cleansing is the finishing of the mystery of God, Revelation 10:7, and the close of probation; and that it is for this reason, among others, a work of Judgment, marvelously simplifies some otherwise very perplexing questions, and makes room for some plainly predicted and necessary events which, on any other view, are not possible.—RH, Nov. 22, 1881.

Smith then looked at ten specific examples and their relation to the sanctuary and its cleansing in 1844:

> 1. It makes provision for a preliminary work of Judgment, which must take place before Christ appears. The least reflection will convince any one that when Christ reveals Himself in the clouds of heaven, there is no time given for the investigation of character, and the work of deciding who are worthy of the blessings He comes to

bring; but He declares that His reward is with Him, to give every man as his work shall be; hence it must have been determined before this what every man's reward is to be; and therefore, as soon as He appears, all the dead in Christ can be raised, while all the wicked dead are still left in their graves, and all the righteous living can be changed in a moment, in the twinkling of an eye. . . .

2. It provides a time and place for Christ to confess before the Father and the holy angels the names of His friends, and deny those of His enemies. Matt. 10:32, 33. . . .

3. It provides a time and place for a blotting out of sins before Christ comes, as in Acts 3:19, 20, or the blotting out of names from the book of life, as in Rev. 3:5. . . .

4. It guards against the error of continually setting times for the Lord to come, inasmuch as it shows that no prophetic period reaches to that event—the longest and latest, the 2300 days—reaching not to the coming of the Lord, but to a work called the cleansing of the sanctuary, which must be accomplished before He comes.

5. It enables us to distinguish between the work of Christ as an offering for sin, and His work as a High Priest atoning for sin. . . .

6. It establishes the doctrine of the immutability of the law and the perpetuity of the Sabbath, by bringing to view in the temple of God in Heaven, under the sounding of the seventh angel, the ark of His [God's] testament. Rev. 11:19. . . .

7. It establishes the doctrine of the soon coming of Christ; for Christ comes as soon as He has finished His work as priest, and He is now performing the closing service of that priestly work. His coming must therefore be at hand.

8. It establishes the doctrine of the unconscious state of the dead, by showing that no part of the Judgment, which must precede the bestowal of rewards and punishments, could be performed till Christ reached the closing division of His work as Mediator. Men and women have not, therefore, through all the ages past, been going to Heaven and hell, but are resting in their graves, awaiting the decision in their cases.

9. It gives us more clear, definite, and beautiful views of Christ's position and work than can be evolved from any other subject.

10. Finally, it sets the seal of divine truth, and of divine providence, to the message now going forth. Here we see the open door which no man can shut. Revelation 3:8. Through this, the ark of God's testament is seen in the temple in Heaven, and no one can shut off the view. Rev. 11:19.—*Ibid.*

In Conclusion

The pioneers, as we have seen, rejected as unscriptural three definitions of the sanctuary. They could not accept it as (1) the earth (a common interpretation among Millerites before October 22, 1844, and strongly believed by many afterward); (2) the church; or (3) Canaan.

The pioneers, rather, regarded the sanctuary as in heaven, and as real as Christ Himself. They believed it inseparably connected with the Sabbath, the state of the dead, the second coming of Christ, and other doctrines. It helps explain the fact that those in the Seventh-day Adventist Church who reject its sanctuary belief have usually found themselves discarding other beliefs, and eventually separating from the church altogether.

* * * *

Ellen White writes on the identity of the two sanctuaries in the following references:

Earthly
Early Writings, pp. 252, 253; *The Great Controversy*, pp. 409-422; *Patriarchs and Prophets*, pp. 343-358; *Spiritual Gifts*, vol. 4a, pp. 5-11; *The Story of Redemption*, pp. 151-157.

Heavenly
Early Writings, pp. 32, 33, 36, 42, 43, 48, 54-56, 86, 243, 244, 250-256, 260, 261, 279-281; *The Great Controversy*, pp. 324-329, 351-353, 398-400, 409-436; *Life Sketches*, pp. 100, 101; *Patriarchs and Prophets*, pp. 343, 351-358; *The Story of Redemption*, pp. 375-381.

* * * *

ARTICLES QUOTED IN THIS CHAPTER

James White
  June 9, 1851, The Parable, Matthew 25:1-12
  Feb. 17, 1852, The Work of Grace
  March 17, 1853, The Sanctuary
  Dec. 5, 1854, The Sanctuary
  March 1, 1870, Our Faith and Hope—The Sanctuary
J. N. Andrews
  Jan. 6, 1853, The Sanctuary
  Aug. 28, 1853, The Antitypical Tabernacle
Uriah Smith
  Jan. 9, 1855, The Sanctuary
  Feb. 11, 1858, Synopsis of the Present Truth (Series)
  Feb. 18, 1858, Synopsis of the Present Truth
  June 22, 1876, The Sanctuary
  Nov. 22, 1881, The Great Central Subject
Roswell F. Cottrell
  July 24, 1855, Too Literal
O. R. L. Crosier
  Feb. 7, 1846, The Law of Moses (*Day-Star Extra*)

3

Entering the Most Holy Place in 1844

Though O. R. L. Crosier provided the first extended discussions of Christ entering the Most Holy Place in the *Day-Dawn* during the winter of 1845-1846 and the *Day-Star* in 1846, written comments on the subject appear almost immediately after the disappointment in 1844. Enoch Jacobs, though he later joined the Shakers, wrote in the Millerite paper that "it seems quite probable that the *coming out* of the High Priest on the 'day of atonement' was typical of Christ sitting in judgment, rather than of His personally appearing to the inhabitants of the earth."—*The Western Midnight Cry*, Nov. 29, 1844.

He reasoned that "it seems necessary that there should be some movement on His part in putting away the sins of His people as a body, before He *personally* appears."—*Ibid.* Therefore, "when Christ personally appears to the inhabitants of the world it is not to sit in judgment and pass sentence upon them: but to execute the judgment previously written."—*Ibid.* Consequently, "our mistakes have not been in wrong calculation of *time* so much as the proper application of events."—*Ibid.*

Anointing Heaven's Sanctuary

Our spiritual forefathers quickly agreed on certain points regarding the sanctuary, including a belief that Christ's activity as High Priest in heaven began in the *holy place* at His ascension, and moved to the *Most Holy Place* in 1844. But before we consider that work, we should observe an important point that confuses some. White, Andrews, and Smith assumed that when He returned to heaven, Christ anointed the *entire* sanctuary—a service foreshadowed by Moses and Aaron when they dedicated the Old

43

Testament tabernacle. After its anointing Aaron began his high priestly service in the holy place. A similar event accompanied the dedication of the later temples. So it was, White and Andrews said, with Christ in heaven.

Still the two men did not confuse the anointing of the sanctuary—including the Most Holy Place—with the work of the high priest that was to follow, namely the daily service in the holy place. Commenting on the anointing portrayed in Daniel 9:24, J. N. Andrews quoted several scholars:

> That this "Most Holy" is the true tabernacle in which the Messiah is to officiate as priest we offer the following testimony: " 'And to anoint the Most Holy;' *kodash kodashim,* the Holy of holies."—Adam Clark. Dan. 9:24.
>
> "Seventy weeks are determined upon thy people, and the city of thy sanctuary: that sin may be restrained, and transgression have an end; that iniquity may be expiated, and an everlasting righteousness brought in; that visions and prophecies may be sealed up, and the Holy of holies anointed."—Houbigant's translation of Dan. 9:24, as cited in Clark's Commentary.
>
> " 'To anoint the Most Holy.' Hebrew, literally 'Holy of holies.' Heaven itself, which Christ consecrated, when He ascended and entered it, sprinkling or consecrating it with His own blood for us."—*Litch's Restitution,* p. 89.*
>
> "And the last event of the 70 weeks, as enumerated in verse 24, was the anointing of the 'Most Holy,' or the 'Holy of Holies,' or the 'Sanctum Sanctorum.' Not that which was on earth, made with hands, but the true tabernacle, heaven itself, into which Christ, our high priest, is for us entered. Christ was to do in the true tabernacle, in heaven, what Moses and Aaron did in its pattern. See Heb. 6; 7; 8; 9. And Ex. 30:22-30. Also Lev. 8:10-15."—*Advent Shield,* No. 1, p. 75.†
> —RH, Jan. 20, 1853.

Andrews reminded his readers that when Christ returned to heaven, He became the minister of the sanctuary, it was anointed, and He presented His sacrifice. "As the ministration of the earthly tabernacle began with its anointing, so in the more excellent ministry of our great High Priest, the first act, as shown to Daniel, is the anointing of the true tabernacle or sanctuary of which He is a minister. Ex. 40:9-11; Lev. 8:10, 11; Num. 7:1; Dan. 9:24.

"It is therefore an established fact that the worldly sanctuary of the first covenant, and the heavenly sanctuary of the new covenant, are both embraced in the vision of the 2300 days. Seventy weeks are

---

* Josiah Litch was a Millerite.
† The *Advent Shield* was a pre-Disappointment Millerite publication.

cut off upon the earthly sanctuary, and at their termination the true tabernacle, with its anointing, its sacrifice and its minister, are introduced."—*Ibid.*

James White also spoke on the topic. "The anointing of the most holy place at the commencement of His [Christ's] ministration, may be urged as proof that He ministers only in the second apartment of the heavenly sanctuary. Dan. 9:24. But this objection vanishes at once, if we consider that before the Levitical priesthood began to minister in the earthly sanctuary, that entire building, the holiest as well as the holy place and all the sacred vessels, was anointed. Ex. 40:9-11; 30:23-29; Lev. 8:10; Num. 7:1. And when this anointing was accomplished, that ministration *began* in the *first* apartment. Lev. 8-10; Heb. 9:6, 7. And this order, let it be remembered, was 'the example and shadow of heavenly things.' "—RH, March 15, 1870.

At the Father's Right Hand

Opponents have accused Seventh-day Adventists of limiting Christ to the holy place for hundreds of years after He returned to heaven. But the pioneers did not hold such a position. James White stated in 1850 that "some take the ground that Jesus entered the Most Holy Place when He ascended to heaven, because He is represented to be at God's right hand. Now I think that no one will contend that Jesus has been perfectly stationary, at the Father's right hand literally, for more than 1800 years."—*The Present Truth,* May, 1850.

He then reminded his readers that "in the typical Sanctuary, God manifested His glory in the Holy, as well as in the Most Holy. So in the Heavenly Sanctuary, Jesus can 'appear in the presence of God for us' in the Holy Place, as well as in the Most Holy. God's throne is above the cherubims, and His glory can be seen from either side of the second vail." *

"The candid Bible reader will see that such expressions of Scripture, as 'right hand of the throne,' 'right hand of God,' 'right hand of power,' mean that Christ, who was humbled to the cross, rose from the dead in triumph, and ascended in glory, and is the next in power to the Eternal God."—*Ibid.*

Uriah Smith contended that the Bible expressions "right hand of the throne," "right hand of God," and "right hand of power" did not

---

* Ellen White speaks of watching in vision both the Father and the Son move from the holy place to the Most Holy Place (see *Early Writings*, pp. 54, 55).

intend to represent *physical* location as much as honor or respect. J. N. Andrews, a few years later spoke to the point when he said that "Christ, as our high priest, or intercessor, sits at the right hand of the Father's throne, *i.e.*, He occupies the place of honor in the presence of One greater, till He is Himself crowned king, when He takes His own throne."—RH, Dec. 7, 1869.

Andrews elaborated further Christ's "position" in heaven, observing that He obviously moved around a great deal.

> The position of the Saviour as high priest cannot be one invariable, fixed posture of sitting. Indeed, although Mark says (chap. 16:19) concerning our Lord "that he was received up into heaven, and sat on the right hand of God," yet it is said of Stephen that "he, being full of the Holy Ghost, looked up stedfastly into heaven, and saw the glory of God, and Jesus *standing* on the right hand of God, and said, Behold, I see the heavens opened, and the Son of man *standing* on the right hand of God." Acts 7:55, 56.
>
> Sometime after this, Saul of Tarsus had an actual interview with Christ, that like the other apostles he might be a *witness in person* to the fact of His *resurrection*. 1 Cor. 9:1; 15:8; Acts 9:3-5, 17, 27; 22:6-8, 14; 26:15, 16.
>
> The fact that Stephen saw our Lord *standing* at His Father's right hand; and that after this, Jesus did *personally appear* to Saul to constitute him a witness of His resurrection, which, in order to be an apostle, he must be, is not inconsistent with the mandate of the Father, "Sit thou at my right hand, until I make thine enemies thy footstool."—*Ibid.*

Looking at both the Old and New Testament meanings of *sit*, Andrews drew some further conclusions:

> The Hebrew word *yahshav*, rendered *sit* in Psalm 110:1, is used an immense number of times in the Old Testament, and is in a very large portion of these cases rendered *dwell*. Thus (Gen. 13:12) "Abram *dwelled* in the land of Canaan, and Lot *dwelled* in the cities of the plain." Again (Gen. 45:10), "And thou shalt *dwell* in the land of Goshen." Also, "David *dwelt* in the country of the Philistines." 1 Sam. 27:7. These examples could be extended to great length. And kindred uses of the word are very numerous. But it is to be observed that Abraham, and Lot, and Jacob, and David, the persons spoken of in these texts who *dwelled*, or as rendered in Psalm 110:1, who *sat* in the places named, were not, during the time in which they acted thus, immovably fixed to those several places, but were capable of going and returning during the very time in question.
>
> And the Greek word *kathizo*, used in the New Testament for Christ's act of sitting at the Father's right hand, though more generally used in the sense of sitting, is also used precisely like *yahshav* in the texts above. Thus it is used in Acts 18:11, where it is said of Paul, that "he *continued* there [at Corinth] a year and six months." But though that was Paul's abiding place during that period, it is every

way probable that he visited other places for occasional preaching during the time.—*Ibid.*

Finally, he referred to Christ's promise to the disciples before He left them:

> When our Lord went away, it was not simply that He should act as intercessor for His people. He also had another work to do. He says: "In my Father's house are many mansions; if it were not so, I would have told you. I go to *prepare* a *place* for you. And if I go and *prepare* a *place* for you, I will come again, and receive you unto myself: that where I am, there ye may be also." We cannot doubt that this work is wrought under our Lord's personal inspection; and it is performed during the period that He is at the Father's right hand.—*Ibid.*

Two Holy Places in Heaven's Sanctuary

In 1853 Andrews presented four Bible evidences that heaven's sanctuary has *two* holy places:

> 1. The tabernacle erected by Moses, after a forty days' inspection of the one showed to him in the mount, consisted of two holy places [Ex. 26:30-33], and is declared to be a correct pattern or model of that building. Ex. 25:8, 9, 40; compared with Chap. 39:32-43. But if the earthly sanctuary consisted of two holy places, and the great original from which it was copied, consisted of only one, instead of likeness, there would be perfect dissimilarity.
>
> 2. The temple was built in every respect according to the pattern which God gave to David by the Spirit. 1 Chron. 28:10-19. . . . The temple was built on a larger and grander scale than the tabernacle; but its distinguishing feature, like the tabernacle, consisted in the fact that it was composed of two holy places. 1 Kings 6; 2 Chron. 3. This is clear proof that the heavenly tabernacle contains the same.
>
> 3. Paul plainly states that "the holy places [plural] made with hands" "are the figures [plural] of the true." And that tabernacle, and its vessels, are "patterns [plural] of things in the heavens." Heb. 9:23, 24. This is direct evidence that, in the greater and more perfect tabernacle, there are two holy places, even as in the "figure," "example" or "pattern."
>
> 4. The apostle actually used the word holies [plural] in speaking of the heavenly sanctuary. The expression "holiest of all," in Hebrews 9:8; 10:19, has been supposed by some to prove that Christ began to minister in the most holy place at His ascension. But the expression is not *"hagia hagion,"* holy of holies, as in chapter 9:3, but is simply *"hagion"* holies. It is the same word that is rendered sanctuary in Hebrews 8:2. In each of these three texts [Heb. 8:2; 9:8; 10:19], Macknight renders the word, "holy places." The Douay Bible renders it "the holies." And thus we learn that the heavenly sanctuary consists of two "holy places."—RH, Feb. 3, 1853.

Does Christ Minister Only in the Holiest?

Millerites expected fire to cleanse the earth as Christ returned.

Disagreement about what happened on October 22 of that year obviously arose afterward. J. N. Andrews reviewed two articles that appeared April 16 and 30, 1853, in *The Advent Herald*, a journal published by Sunday-observing Adventists.

"The *Herald* freely admits the ministration of the Levitical priesthood in both the holy places of the earthly tabernacle, and, also, that the greater, and more perfect tabernacle in heaven has taken the place of that pattern," he commented. "But it contends (if we do not mistake its meaning) that the holiest of all is the only part of the earthly tabernacle that was a pattern of the true tabernacle in heaven; and that the ministration in that apartment was the only part of the ministration in the earthly tabernacle that prefigured the ministration of Christ in heaven; and that, unlike the earthly high priest, who cleansed the Sanctuary at the close of his ministration, because the sins of the people had been borne there, our High Priest cleanses the heavenly Sanctuary at the very commencement of His ministry, and preparatory to His act of making intercession for us."—RH, May 12, 1853.

But Andrews did not agree with their conclusions. Turning to the Bible, he raised several objections:

> From these views of the *Herald* we dissent, for the following reasons:
>
> 1. Because the entire building, *viz:* the two holy places (and not merely the holiest of all), is expressly stated to be the pattern of the true tabernacle. (1) Moses, at the command of God, made a tabernacle consisting of two holy places, after the pattern showed to him in the Mount. Ex. 25:8, 9; 26:33. (2) David received the *pattern* of the temple "by the Spirit"; and Solomon erected the temple consisting of two holy places, after that pattern. 1 Chron. 28:10-19; 2 Chron. 3. (3) Paul testifies that these holy places were the figures [plural] of the true, and patterns of things in the heavens. Heb. 9:23, 24. (4) The word rendered Sanctuary [Heb. 8:2] and the Holiest of all [Chap. 9:8; 10:19], is plural signifying holies, or holy places; thus furnishing incontrovertible testimony that the heavenly Sanctuary does not consist merely, of the holiest of all.
>
> 2. We dissent from the position of the *Herald* that the ministration in the holiest of all was the only part of the work of the earthly priests that typified the work of our Lord in the heavenly tabernacle. (1) We know of no evidence to sustain such a view. (2) It is expressly stated that the ministration of the priests under the typical dispensation was "the shadow of good things to come"; "the *example* and *shadow* of heavenly things"; and that Christ ministers in the greater and more perfect tabernacle, a High Priest of those good things to come. Heb. 8:5; 9:11; 10:1. (3) The holiest of all, containing the ark of God's

testament is not opened until the sounding of the seventh angel.* Rev. 11:19.—*Ibid.*

Clearly Andrews believed that the heavenly sanctuary had more than one apartment. He saw the position of Sunday-observing Adventists as *reversing* the work of Christ:

> We think these facts do completely disprove the view that there is but one apartment to the tabernacle in heaven, and that our Lord is a minister simply of one holy place. If we are correct in believing that the ministration in the earthly tabernacle was "the *example* and *shadow*" of Christ's more excellent ministry, then it is a certainty that Christ does not *exactly reverse* the order of that ministration! In other words, as the work of the earthly priest was *concluded* by the act of cleansing the Sanctuary, and placing the sins, thus removed from it, upon the head of the scape-goat, we may not expect our High Priest to *begin* His work in the heavenly tabernacle by that act. If so, the work in the earthly tabernacle, instead of being the example and shadow of Christ's work, is exactly the reverse of it.
>
> Nor is there the least intimation in Paul's commentary on the types, that the cleansing of the Sanctuary is to be before the Lord Jesus ministers in that building for our sins. On the contrary, Paul shows that the heavenly Tabernacle was to be cleansed for the same reason that the earthly Sanctuary had been, *viz:* Because the sins of the people had been borne there. Heb. 9:23, 24. This fact incontrovertibly proves that the cleansing of the heavenly Sanctuary, like that of the earthly, occurs at the conclusion of the ministration therein.—*Ibid.*

The Daily Service

Some years later Andrews went into careful detail about the distinct services conducted in the sanctuary. Considering the daily ritual, he wrote that "the ministration in the first apartment occupied the entire year, with the exception of one day, which was devoted to work in the second apartment, or most holy place, to close up the work which had been wrought in the first apartment. The work in the first apartment was on this wise: When a man repented of his sin he brought a sin offering to the priest at the door of the sanctuary. Then he confessed his sin to the priest, and put his hand upon the head of his offering to indicate the transfer of the guilt from himself to his offering.

"Then the victim was slain because of that guilt thus transferred to it, and the blood, representing the life of the victim, was taken by the priest and carried into the sanctuary and sprinkled there before God. This act was the offering of the life of an innocent victim in the

---

* Ellen White often used Revelation 11:19 in support of an investigative judgment. On January 5, 1849, however, she saw in vision that the events of Revelation 11:18 were yet future (see *Early Writings,* p. 36).

place of the life of him who had broken the law of God, and it was the transference of that man's guilt from himself to the sanctuary of God. See Leviticus 4 and the parallel scriptures. This was the most important feature of the work in the first apartment, and by it the guilt of the penitents was transferred from themselves to the tabernacle."—RH, March 10, 1874.

The Yearly Service

Next he examined the yearly service. "On the tenth day of the seventh month, which was called the day of atonement, the ministration was transferred to the second apartment, or most holy place. Lev. 16. By God's direction, the high priest on this day caused two goats to be brought to the door of the sanctuary. On these he was to cast lots. One was for the Lord, the other was for Azazel. Then he slew the goat upon which the Lord's lot fell, and took his blood to present it before God as a sin offering in the most holy place, sprinkling it upon the mercy seat. He did this for two purposes: 1. To make atonement for the people. 2. To cleanse the sanctuary by removing from it the sins of the people of God. Lev. 16:15-19.

"The sanctuary being cleansed, the high priest comes out of the building, and having caused the other goat to be brought, which was for Azazel, he lays both his hands upon his head, and confesses over him all the transgressions of the children of Israel in all their sins. These he puts upon the head of the goat and sends him away by the hand of a fit man into the wilderness. And it is said that 'the goat shall bear upon him all their iniquities unto a land not inhabited.' Verses 20-22."—*Ibid.*

Christ Began in the Holy Place

Andrews offered evidence that Christ began His work at His ascension in the holy place of heaven's sanctuary. "When John looked into the temple of God in Heaven, he saw the Father sitting upon the throne, and before the throne were seven lamps burning. Rev. 4. In this place also he saw the Son of God. Rev. 5. Before the throne also stood the golden altar of incense. Rev. 8:3. These things do clearly mark the first apartment of the heavenly sanctuary, and show that this was the place where our Lord began His ministration as our High Priest."—*Ibid.*

Finally, he pointed to scriptural indications that at a certain point in time, Christ changed His ministry in heaven to the Most Holy Place.

"As there was a time each year devoted to the finishing up of the round of service in 'the *example* and *shadow* of heavenly things' so is there such a period in the conclusion of Christ's ministration, when once for all, our High Priest finishes His work of priesthood; and as this work in the former dispensation took place in the second apartment, so also under the new convenant does this work find its accomplishment within the second vail by the ark of the ten commandments. The work in the second apartment of the earthly sanctuary does not therefore represent the work of the whole gospel dispensation, but only of that part of it devoted to the finishing of the mystery of God.—*Ibid.*

Contention With Sunday-observing Adventists

Contention over the *place* of Christ's beginning ministry continued between Sunday-observing Adventists and Seventh-day Adventists for many years. J. N. Loughborough and James White held evangelistic meetings in Portland, Maine, late in 1858, and after one session, Sunday-observing Adventists there asked for a Bible study to examine the sanctuary. Both Loughborough and White wrote accounts for the *Review.* "It was proposed by some of the Advent friends in that city, who do not see as we do on all points," White commented, "that we have a Bible class, if agreeable to us. Most cheerfully we accepted the proposition."—RH, Jan. 13, 1859.

The non-Sabbatarian Adventists insisted that Christ had begun His ministry in the Most Holy Place in heaven immediately after His ascension:

> During the evening the following texts were presented as proof that Christ entered the Most Holy Place and commenced His ministry there at the time of His ascension to heaven.
> Heb. 9:8. "The Holy Ghost this signifying, that the way into the holiest of all was not yet made manifest, while as the first tabernacle was yet standing."
> Chap. 10:19. "Having therefore, brethren, boldness to enter into the holiest by the blood of Jesus."—*Ibid.*

Loughborough called their attention to another translation by MacKnight that rendered the word *holiest* as "holies" or "holy places." "But this translation was rejected, with the singular and uncalled-for assertion, 'I shall not give up my Bible.' "—*Ibid.*

White next turned to Loughborough's argument for two apartments in heaven's sanctuary. "Brother L. called attention to Hebrews 9:3. 'And after the *second* vail, the tabernacle which is called the holiest of all.' As a second implies a first, Paul understood that there were two vails. Christ entered within the first of these vails when He ascended."—*Ibid.*

White then commented that his readers should "judge of our surprise when the very persons who a few moments before had rejected Macknight's translation, saying, 'I shall not give up my Bible,' now suggested that Paul's statement concerning the second vail, must be a misprint, or wrong translation!!! The wrong side of a question is generally the hard side; and those who are on that side, and are determined to maintain their position, are sometimes driven to say things which contradict themselves."—*Ibid.*

The session ended with no clear resolution of the difficulty. James White said that "we were left to conclude that their position, if indeed they had a position, was that the earth is the holy place, heaven the most holy, and the ethereal blue was the vail between!! This we know is the vague view which many take of the subject."—*Ibid.*

In 1875 Smith expressed his conviction that Satan himself attempted to create confusion as to where Jesus went upon His return to heaven. "As is perhaps natural, the enemy of truth seems most persistent in trying to trouble and unsettle minds in reference to the sanctuary; for that is the citadel of our strength; and the special point of attack is the idea that the cleansing of the sanctuary began, by the entrance of Christ into the most holy place, at the end of the 2300 days in 1844. Hence his scheme to make men believe that Christ entered the most holy place when He ascended."—RH, Aug. 5, 1875.

Hebrews 6:19, 20

Opposition to the Seventh-day Adventist understanding that Christ went to the holy place at His ascension has frequently used Hebrews 6:19, 20 to support that contention. Uriah Smith spoke to the point:

> Paul's testimony in Hebrews 6:19, 20, is quoted to prove that when Christ ascended He entered into the most holy place: "Which hope we have as an anchor of the soul, both sure and steadfast, and which entereth into that within the vail; whither the forerunner is for us entered, even Jesus, made an high priest forever after the order of Melchisedec."
>
> The claim here instituted is that "the vail," within which Christ has entered, signifies the vail dividing between the holy and most holy places; and if Christ entered within that vail when He ascended, or if He was there when Paul wrote, He was in the most holy place.
>
> If we grant this claim, some conclusions follow which demand consideration. If there is a vail dividing between the holy and the most

holy places, which the foregoing claim admits, then there is somewhere a holy place as well as a most holy. But if the most holy is all Heaven where Christ has entered, then what and where is the holy place? It must be something outside of Heaven. Then what is it? Is it this earth, as some contend? If it is anything outside of Heaven it must be; for this is the only place with which we have anything to do this side of Heaven.—RH, July 20, 1876.

He pointed out some additional problems with such a view:

The holy place in the sanctuary was twice as large as the most holy; and if the earth is the holy place of the true sanctuary, and Heaven the most holy, it follows, the proportion being maintained, that this little diminutive earth, of which it would take three hundred and fifty-two thousand to equal the bulk of the sun, is twice as large as all Heaven!

And still further, in fulfillment of the type, Christ must perform a portion of His ministry in the holy place. If this is the earth, He should have performed a portion of His ministry here.—*Ibid.*

Then he offered a Biblical answer to the dilemma:

But Paul says explicitly that He could not be a priest upon the earth; for there was another order of priests appointed to do all the work of this kind that was to be done on the earth. Heb. 8:4. And he says again that while the earthly tabernacle stood, while any service of that kind was performed here, the way into the holy places, both the holy and the most holy of the heavenly sanctuary, was not made manifest or laid open. Heb. 9:8.—*Ibid.*

The Veil in Hebrews 6:19

Smith explored further the meaning of the veil in Hebrews 6:19. Going again to the Bible, he offered the following suggestions:

Why call the vail in Hebrews 6:19 the second vail? Simply to avoid the conclusion that the Lord is doing any special work either in Heaven or on earth at the present time; for if the sanctuary is not now being cleansed, the position and work of our Lord differ in no respect from what they have been the past 1800 years; and the past advent movement is all a failure. But if there is nothing to the past movement, there is certainly nothing to the present. Thus men labor hard to give the devil the whole field, and exhibit themselves as the victims of the thinnest of all delusions.

We inquire, then, Does the word "vail" in Hebrews 6:19 mean the second vail? We answer, No; and this we will prove to the satisfaction of every candid mind. There are but two words rendered vail in the New Testament. These are καλυμμα and καταπετασμα. The first occurs four times only, in verse 13, 14, 15 and 16 of 2 Corinthians 3, referring to the vail over Moses' face. The second is used six times, once each by Matthew, Mark and Luke, all in reference to the vail of the temple which was rent in twain when Christ expired upon the cross, Matt. 27:51; Mark 15:38; Luke 23:45; and three times by Paul in the book of Hebrews: 6:19; 9:3; and 10:20.

Is there anything peculiar in Paul's use of this word in Hebrews? Yes; when he means the second vail he specifies it. Heb. 9:3: "And after the *second* vail, the tabernacle which is called the holiest of all." Now if the term "the vail" was used to signify invariably the second vail, why did Paul use the term *second*? Why did he not say, here, simply, "And after the vail"? Because a second must imply a first, and he well understood that there was at the entrance to the tabernacle a hanging, which was just as much a vail as that which divided between the holy and the most holy; and to carry out his purpose of instruction in reference to the sanctuary, which is one of Paul's great objects in the book of Hebrews, he accurately distinguishes between the two, and when he means the second, he says the second.—*Ibid.*

Between the Cherubims

In a following article, Smith expressed belief that God's throne was not always in a fixed place.

> And still another attempt is made to find an objection to the view we advocate, that Christ commenced His ministry as priest in the first apartment of the sanctuary in Heaven when He ascended up on high. It is framed on this wise: God is spoken of as dwelling between the cherubim. These cherubim were on the ends of the mercy seat which was the cover of the ark; and the ark was always in the most holy place, or second apartment of the sanctuary. This, therefore, being God's fixed location, when Christ ascended up to the right hand of the Father on high, He of necessity entered where God was, into the most holy place, and hence did not commence His ministry in the holy place.
>
> The passages which contain the expression "Between the cherubims" are the following: Ex. 25:22; Num. 7:89; 1 Sam. 4:4; 2 Sam. 6:2; 2 Kings 19:15; Isa. 37:16; Ps. 80:1; 99:1; Eze. 10:2, 6, 7.—RH, July 27, 1876.

Smith did not accept that the passages supported the position that Christ went directly to the Most Holy Place in heaven at His ascension.

> Before these passages can be made available for our opponents, it must be shown,
>
> First, That God immovably fixed Himself to that position between the cherubim on the ark, and did not meet or commune with His people from any other place. But this is contrary to the record; for at times He met both with Moses and the children of Israel at the door of the tabernacle. Ex. 29:42, 43; 33:9, 10. And again, was God dwelling between the cherubim of the ark when the sons of Eli rashly took it out to battle, and it fell into the hands of the Philistines? It must be shown,
>
> Secondly, That even though God did meet and commune with His

servants from between the cherubim of the ark here below, so much so that it is spoken of as His dwelling place, it must also be so in Heaven. But this would not inevitably follow; for in His intercourse with men this might be the best mode of procedure, but not necessarily so in Heaven. It must be shown,

Thirdly, That the cherubim between whom God dwells on high are the cherubim of the ark. But this cannot be shown; for it appears from Ezekiel's vision of God and His throne, in Ezekiel, chapters 1 and 10, that the throne of God itself is a living throne, supported by the most exalted order of cherubim. And the most appropriate representation of this fact that could be given here on earth was to designate the locality between the cherubim over the ark, as His dwelling place in His ordinary intercourse with the human race. It must be shown,

Fourthly, That God's throne in Heaven is immovably fixed to one place. But this cannot be shown; for in Ezekiel's vision above referred to it is represented as full of awful life and unapproachable majesty, and moving whithersoever the Spirit was to go. And as in the earthly tabernacle, so here, it sometimes stood at the door of the Lord's house. Eze. 10:18, 19. It must be shown,

Fifthly, That the declaration that Christ ascended to the right hand of the throne of the majesty in the Heavens, signifies locality, rather than position in respect to exaltation and power. But this cannot be shown; for even when Christ appears coming in the clouds of heaven, He is said to be sitting on the right hand of power. Matt. 27:64.—*Ibid.*

Consequently, Smith felt that "the argument of our opponents fails them at every step."—*Ibid.*

One further observation would be in order from Smith. Writing in 1888, he spoke of how a one-apartment sanctuary in heaven would create an incomplete type for the earthly sanctuary. "If the heavenly sanctuary has but one apartment, corresponding to the most holy place, and Christ ministers only therein, it follows that two thirds of the sanctuary, as constructed by Moses (the holy place) was an unwarrantable addition, and had no antitype, and that all the service of the priests through the entire year, except one solitary day, was performed unto the example and shadow of nothing! Such teaching is an insult to the sacred record."—RH, April 17, 1888.

In Conclusion

It did not take long for the pioneers to arrive at the firm conviction that instead of coming to the earth to cleanse it with fire in 1844, Christ had entered the Most Holy Place in heaven's sanctuary to begin a final judgment of those who professed to be

His people.

Three important parallels were clear to them. When Christ returned to heaven after His resurrection, He (1) became the High Priest of the sanctuary there, as Aaron and others who followed him were high priests of earth's sanctuary in Old Testament times; (2) He (in the view of White and Smith) anointed the entire heavenly sanctuary as was done at the construction of the Old Testament sanctuary; and (3) He began His work in the holy place even as the high priest in Old Testament times first performed the daily service in the holy place, and followed that ministration with the yearly service in the Most Holy Place, known as the Day of Atonement.

The pioneers also saw that Christ was not limited as to locality in heaven. He had a variety of work to do, and was sometimes involved in ministering to those on earth as well as preparing mansions for those finally saved.

It was clear to them that heaven's sanctuary has two apartments just as the one on earth did in Old Testament times. If Christ was to be truly represented by the Old Testament priests, His service in heaven must have two phases: (1) His ministration in the holy place for a certain period, and (2) His final one in the Most Holy Place.

* * * *

Ellen White wrote of Christ entering the Most Holy Place in 1844 in the following references:

The Great Controversy, pp. 423-426, 479-491.
Early Writings, pp. 55, 243, 251, 280.
The Story of Redemption, p. 379.

* * * *

ARTICLES QUOTED IN THIS CHAPTER

Enoch Jacobs
 Nov. 29, 1844, Evidence . . . for the Tenth Day of the Seventh Month *(Midnight Cry)*
James White
 May, 1850, The Sanctuary, 2300 Days, and Shut Door *(Present Truth)*
 Jan. 13, 1859, The Sanctuary
 March 15, 1870, Our Faith and Hope—The Heavenly Sanctuary (Series)
J. N. Andrews
 Jan. 20, 1853, The Sanctuary
 Feb. 3, 1853, The Sanctuary
 May 12, 1853, The Cleansing of the Sanctuary
 Dec. 7, 1869 The Order of Events in the Judgment
 March 10, 1874, The Sanctuary of the Bible
Uriah Smith
 March 28, 1854, The Sanctuary (Series)
 Aug. 5, 1875, Questions on the Sanctuary
 July 20, 1876, The Sanctuary (Series)
 July 27, 1876, The Sanctuary (Series)
 April 17, 1888, Not the Very Image

4

The Year-Day Principle in Prophecy

Students of Bible prophecy have not all agreed as to methods of prophetic interpretation. The pioneers took the historical approach in their study. Other schools of interpretation—such as futurist and preterist—developed during the Catholic counterreformation. Most Protestant interpreters, as well as Millerites, followed the historical method. We could briefly characterize the three methods as follows:

1. *Preterist.* The prophecies of Daniel had their accomplishment no later than the first century A.D. and those of the book of Revelation by the fifth century A.D.

2. *Futurist.* The seventieth week of Daniel 9 and the bulk of the prophecies of Revelation apply to the end of the age, and are yet to happen.

3. *Historical.* (The Adventist approach generally.) The unrolling of the historical events from the times of Daniel and John until the second coming of Christ combine to fulfill prophecy.

The Biblical key to the 2300 day prophecy of Daniel 8:14 was extremely important to the Adventist pioneers. They considered it of the highest priority to establish with confidence that the year-day principle was valid for calculating prophetic time. William Miller and all the Adventist preachers prior to October 22, 1844, built their faith on it. But would it stand the test of the Disappointment?

Obviously, Christ had not come as predicted according to their calculation of the prophecy. Did their arithmetic contain some error? Was the year-day principle false? What had *really* happened in 1844? These are important questions. Some we have already

57

considered. But what was the answer of Adventist pioneers to the question of the year-day principle?

The Seventy Weeks and the Year-Day Principle

Uriah Smith did not join the pioneers of the Seventh-day Adventist Church until near the end of 1852, though he had been among the Millerites while quite young. Yet he was one of the first to write an affirmation of the year-day prophetic concept, discussing the 70-week prophecy of Daniel 9:24, 25 in 1854. "Unto the Messiah the Prince, says the prediction, shall be seven weeks and threescore and two weeks—69 weeks or 483 days. Messiah the Prince is Jesus Christ. Reckoning from 457 B.C., 483 *years* bring us to A.D. 27, where we find Christ commencing His public ministry, preaching the gospel of the kingdom of God, and saying, 'The time is fulfilled.' No time can here be referred to, but the 69 weeks which were then fulfilled. This fixes the fact that the days are prophetic; that is, a day for a year. Num. 14:34; Eze. 4:6. We also see that it harmonizes perfectly with the conditions of the prophecy.—RH, March 21, 1854.

The Meaning of "Day" in Prophecy

Later, as editor of the *Review*, Smith answered a question on the meaning of "day" in Daniel 8:14.

> Brother W. Bruin writes: "I have troubled myself for some time about Daniel 8:14. I could not feel at home with your calculations, and the theory based upon them. I find in the Hebrew not *days*, as in chapter 12:11, 12, *yamin*, but *evening* and *morning (erev boker)*, as in verse 26, where it is literally translated in the English version the evening and the morning. The same we meet in Genesis 1:5; literally, *and it had been (erev) evening, and it had been (boker) morning, the first day!* So we get, according to the original, 1150 literal days! Not prophetic days! How is that?"
>
> On the question here introduced, there are a number of sources from which light may be obtained. If the expression "evening and morning" is synonymous with the word "day," then we can attach to it a prophetic signification, the same as to the latter, and it becomes a matter of complete indifference which is used.
>
> 1. On the definition of these words we find the following in Gesenius: Under the word evening, he gives the expression "evening and morning" *(geh-rev boh-ker,* according to the spelling given in the Hebrew concordance) and defines it, "a day and night, that is, *the civil day of 24 hours.* Dan. 8:14." The word "day" *(yohm)* is defined by the same author as follows: *"Day,* so called from the diurnal heat. Spoken of the natural day from the rising to the setting of the sun, opp. the night; also of the *civil day,* or *24 hours which includes the night."*
>
> 2. Gesenius makes the expression "evening and morning" as above, equivalent to the Greek *nuxthēmeron,* a word which Liddell

and Scott define as meaning, "A day and night, the space of 24 hours."

3. The Greek word for day, *hēmera*, corresponding to the Hebrew *yohm*, is defined by Robinson thus: A day, i.e., the time from one sunrise or sunset to another, the same as *nuxthēmeron*."

4. In Genesis 1:5, we read that the evening and the morning *(geh-rev boh-ker)* were the first day *(yohm)*.

5. Dr. Hales in his *Analysis of Chronology*, vol. 1, p. 10, says: "The earliest measure of Time on record is the *Day*. In that most ancient and venerable account of the Creation by Moses, the process is marked by the operations of each day. The 'evening and the morning were the first day,' etc. Gen. 1:5, etc. Here the word 'day' denotes the civil or calendar day of 24 hours, including the 'evening' or natural night, and 'the morning' or natural day; while the sun is either below or above the horizon of any place, in the course of the earth's diurnal rotation, between two successive appulses of the same meridian to the sun: corresponding, therefore, to a solar day in astronomy.

"It is remarkable, that the *'evening,'* or natural *night*, precedes the *'morning,'* or natural *day*, in the Mosaic account. Hence the Hebrew compound *'Evening-morning'* is used by the prophet Daniel to denote a civil day, in his famous chronological prophecy of the 2300 days, Daniel 8:14. And also the Greek compound *nuxthēmeron*, to denote the same. And hence Hesiod, the eldest of the Greek poets that have reached us, represents the occultation of the *Pleiades* as lasting *nuktas te kai hēmata tessarakonta*, 'forty *nights* and *days*,' i.e., calendar days. And following the primeval order, the ancient Gauls and Germans, counted times and seasons by the number of nights, not of days; as we learn from Caesar and Tacitus; a usage still retained by their descendants; for in old French, *anuit* signifies *'to-day;'* and in English, *sevennight, fortnight*, 'seven days,' 'fourteen days.' Thus is sacred history verified by primitive tradition, handed down to the present times; 'the *night seeming to usher in the day.'*"

6. The Septuagint in Daniel 8:14 expresses the word days in the text, the same as in verses 11 and 12 of chapter 12, showing how the seventy learned Jews understood the original Hebrew, two hundred and eighty-five years before Christ.

From all these authorities, it is impossible to conclude otherwise than that, although the literal Hebrew of Daniel 8:14, is "evening morning," according to the margin, it means precisely the same as though the other expression for day *(yohm)* had there been used. That the expression is symbolic, each day standing for a year, is proved by two considerations: (1) Being in the midst of a symbolic prophecy, the days must be considered symbolic, unless we have the most positive reasons to show that they are literal; which we have not. (2) The days are evidently given to cover very nearly the whole duration of all the kingdoms mentioned in the prophecy; but taken as literal days, amounting to about six years and a half, they would not cover a portion that would be worth mentioning of the existence of even the first empire. They must therefore denote 2300 years, as all expositors agree.—RH, June 12, 1866.

How Long the Vision?

Ten years later Smith again considered the year-day principle in prophecy. He looked at the question asked by the saint in Daniel 8:13—"How long the vision?"

> Now if in reply the angel singled out a period only six years and one third in length, then there is no correspondence either between this answer and the vision in connection with which it was given, or between the answer and the question which directly called it forth. These days if taken literally would be far from covering the duration of any one of the kingdoms of the prophecy taken singly, how much less of them all taken together.
>
> This is symbolic prophecy; it would be natural therefore to conclude that the time introduced would be of a like nature.—RH, Feb. 3, 1876.

Ezekiel and Year-Day

Smith then called attention to a contemporary of Daniel as an illustration of the year-day principle:

> The Bible gives the exact proportion between literal and symbolic time. Ezekiel during the selfsame Babylonish captivity in which Daniel's prophecies were delivered symbolizes *years* by *days*. He was commanded to make known to his fellow exiles by the river Chebar, near the Euphrates, the fate of Jerusalem, with her last king Zedekiah, and also God's reason for it. For this purpose he was to lie prostrate with his face toward the city, on his left side 390 days for Israel, and on his right side 40 days for Judah, restricted all the while to a famine diet, like the Jews he represented shut up in the siege. And God said, I have appointed thee *each day for a year*. Eze. 4:6.
>
> In this representation Ezekiel himself became a symbol. He was acting a symbolic part, an individual representing a nation, the *days* in which he was acting his part symbolizing the actual *years* of the punishment of those whom he represented.—*Ibid.*

Israel and Year-Day

He noted the same principle illustrated in the experience of Israel on the border of Canaan:

> Another instance, not so evidently symbolic in its nature, but equally definite in showing how God uses short periods of time to represent longer ones, and the proportion to be observed between them, is found in Numbers 14:34: "Forty days, each day for a year."—*Ibid.*

History of Year-Day Application

Further, he reminded Adventists that William Miller was not the first to employ the year-day concept in prophecy:

THE YEAR-DAY PRINCIPLE IN PROPHECY

This principle of interpretation, though not the exact application of this prophecy, was adopted by Augustine, Tichonius, Primasius, Andreas, the venerable Bede, Ambrosius, Ansbertus, Berengaud, Bruno Astensis, etc.—*Ibid.*

Smith then made a point that he considered conclusive:

But that which demonstrates beyond question the correctness of the year-day principle is the fact that we, living down in the last years of prophetic fulfillment, are now able to trace out in history the accomplishment of these predictions; and we find that the seventy weeks of Daniel 9, the 1260, 1290, and 1335 days of Daniel 7 and 12, and Revelation 12 and 13, and the five months, and hour, day, month, and year of Revelation 9 have all been exactly fulfilled a day for a year. The 2300 days of Daniel 8:14 are therefore 2300 literal years.—*Ibid.*

The "Days" Are Not Literal

Andrews also explored the year-day principle in prophecy, and supported it. His approach suggested the impossibility of its application in literal time to the great kingdoms of Daniel's vision because of the length of time they remained in power. Looking at the question of time in prophecy, he said:

The prophet learned the duration of his vision. For he heard Gabriel ask Michael, "How long shall be the vision concerning the daily sacrifice, and the transgression of desolation to give both the sanctuary and the host to be trodden under foot?" And Michael, who answered the question to Daniel, said, "Unto two thousand and three hundred days; then shall the sanctuary be cleansed." Verses 13, 14.

Now, it is plain that the period of twenty-three hundred days cannot be understood to mean so many literal days; for this would not make quite seven years, and would cover only a very small part of the duration of one of the three great empires of this vision. . . .

If we compare spiritual things with spiritual, we shall find the key to the interpretation of these days. For the different inspired writers were all led by the same Spirit of truth. They were like so many workmen engaged in building a temple. If we can find the rule which governed one of them, we shall find that same rule governing all the rest in like circumstances. Now God gave this rule to Ezekiel in the interpretation of the symbols of his own vision: "I have appointed thee each day for a year." Eze. 4:6. We shall find in Gabriel's explanation of this vision of Daniel given in the ninth chapter, that the days in Daniel's prophecy are so many years.—RH, March 10, 1874.

In Conclusion

The pioneers believed that Scripture strongly supports the year-day principle. Considering the concept essential to the unique Adventist belief regarding the sanctuary and its cleansing, they believed it to be explicitly stated in the symbolic instructions given to Ezekiel, a contemporary of Daniel, and implied (1) in the symbolic nature of Daniel's vision, (2) in the time lapse of the several kingdoms of the vision, and (3) in the pragmatic tests of fulfillment.

They demonstrated its validity within Daniel's vision itself. From the beginning, Seventh-day Adventists have maintained that the fulfillment of the 70 weeks has precisely demonstrated not only the accuracy of that prophecy but also the validity of the year-day concept in prophecy generally. The balance of the 2300 days inevitably brings us to 1844 and Christ's final work in heaven's sanctuary in the Most Holy Place.

* * * *

Ellen White testifies to her belief in the year-day principle in the following references:

The Great Controversy, pp. 323-329, 340, 457; *Early Writings*, p. 75; *Prophets and Kings*, pp. 554-556.

* * * *

ARTICLES QUOTED IN THIS CHAPTER

J. N. Andrews
March 10, 1874, The Sanctuary of the Bible

Uriah Smith
March 21, 1854, The Sanctuary
June 12, 1866, The 2300 Days
Feb. 3, 1876, The Sanctuary (Series)

5

Seventy Weeks
and 2300 Days

A related question to the year-day principle of prophecy was whether the 70 weeks and 2300 days had a common beginning date. Without exception, pioneer writers held that they did.

Seventy Weeks and 2300 Days—
A Common Beginning

In 1852 J. N. Andrews quoted from a Sunday-observing Adventist journal that "it is by the Canon of Ptolemy that the great prophetical period of seventy weeks is fixed. This Canon places the seventh year of Artaxerxes in the year B.C. 457; and the accuracy of the Canon is demonstrated by the concurrent agreement of more than twenty eclipses.—The seventy weeks date from the going forth of a decree respecting the restoration of Jerusalem.—There were no decrees between the seventh and twentieth years of Artaxerxes. Four hundred and ninety years, beginning with the seventh, must commence in B.C. 457, and end in A.D. 34."—RH, Dec. 23, 1852, quoted from the *Advent Herald*,* March 2, 1850.

After agreeing with their calculations, he continued to the logical conclusion of such figuring. "These important dates are clearly and unequivocally established by historical, chronological and astronomical testimony. Sixty-nine of the seventy weeks from the decree in B.C. 457, ended in A.D. 27, when our Lord was baptized, and began to preach, saying, 'The time is fulfilled.' Mark 1. Three and a half years from this, brings us to the midst of the week in A.D. 31, where it is demonstrated that our Lord was crucified. Three and

---

* Journals published by Sunday-observing and Sabbath-observing Adventists at times had similar titles.

a half years from A.D. 31, the period of seventy weeks terminates in the Autumn of A.D. 34. Or to be more definite the first three and a half years of the seventieth week ended in the first Jewish month [April] in the Spring of A.D. 31. The remaining three and a half years would therefore end in the seventh month, Autumn of A.D. 34.

"Here then we stand at the end of the great period which Gabriel, in explaining the 2300 days to Daniel, tells him was cut off upon Jerusalem and the Jews. Its commencement, intermediate dates, and final termination are unequivocally established. It remains then to notice this one grand fact: the first 490 years of the 2300 ended in the seventh month, Autumn of A.D. 34. This period of 490 years being cut off from the 2300, a period of 1810 years remains. This period of 1810 years being added to the seventh month, Autumn of A.D. 34, brings us to the seventh month, Autumn of 1844. And here, after every effort which has been made to remove the dates, all are compelled to let them stand."—*Ibid.*

Wrong Reasoning Led to Disappointment

Then Andrews summarized the reasons why Millerite Adventists expected Christ to come in 1844:

With these facts before us we reasoned as follows:
(1) The sanctuary is the earth, or the land of Palestine.
(2) The cleansing of the sanctuary is the burning of the earth, or the purification of Palestine, at the coming of Christ.
(3) And hence, we concluded that our Great High Priest would leave the tabernacle of God in heaven and descend in flaming fire, on the tenth day of the seventh month, in the Autumn of 1844.
It is needless to say that we were painfully disappointed. And, though the man does not live who can overthrow the chronological argument, which terminates the 2300 days at that time, or meet the mighty array of evidence by which it is fortified and sustained, yet multitudes, without stopping to inquire whether our conceptions of the sanctuary and of its cleansing were correct or not, have openly denied the agency of Jehovah in the Advent movement, and have pronounced it the work of man.—*Ibid.*

The Changing Position
of Sunday-observing Adventists

But *after* the Disappointment, Sunday-observing Adventists no longer accepted the connection between the seventy weeks and the 2300 days. Andrews quoted from a correspondent to the *Advent Herald* who asked about the seventy weeks and the 2300 days, " 'Must we not henceforth consider that they have different starting points?' " (*ibid.*; quoted from *Advent Herald*, May 22, 1852), and received an affirmative answer from the *Herald's* editor.

To his disappointment, Andrews observed that "not being able to longer maintain a position in denying the termination of the 2300 years in the past, while at the same time they were setting forth an unanswerable vindication of the original dates for the commencement of the period, the *Herald* has at last *denied* the *connection* between the seventy weeks and the 2300 days. We write this with deep regret."—*Ibid.*

James White also mentioned the efforts of Sunday-observing Adventists to separate the two time periods in order to discredit the 1844 date for any important event. "The position of the *Advent Herald,* relative to the 2300 days of Daniel 8, is certainly very unpleasant. The conductors of that paper have formerly maintained the connection between the seventy weeks and the 2300 days, and those who disconnected the two periods have been considered by them, as departing from the 'original Advent faith.' The *Herald* has also ably and fully defended B.C. 457 as the period from which to date the seventy weeks. If both of these positions maintained by the *Herald* are correct, then the 2300 days terminated in 1844, as taught by the *Review*. But the *Herald* objects to this view of the subject, on the ground that the event placed at the end of the 2300 days did not occur. What is that event? Answer: 'Then shall the Sanctuary be cleansed.' Now is there scripture proof that the cleansing of the Sanctuary is the coming of Christ and the burning of the world? We can find none.—RH, Dec. 6, 1853.

Millerite Position Reviewed

Adventist writers during the Millerite period regularly connected Daniel 8 and 9 and the two time periods considered. Uriah Smith noted a few such writers:

> "It is no more proper to say that the ninth chapter of Daniel 'is complete in itself,' than it would be to say that a map which was designed to show the relation of Massachusetts to the United States referred to nothing but Massachusetts. It is no more complete in itself than a bond given in security for a note, or some other document to which it refers, is complete in itself; and we doubt if there is a schoolboy of fourteen in the land, of ordinary capacity, who would not on reading the ninth chapter, with an understanding of the clause before us, decide that it referred to something distinct from itself, called the vision. What vision it is, there is no difficulty in determining. It naturally and obviously refers to the vision which was not fully explained to Daniel, and to which Gabriel calls his attention in the preceding verse—*the vision of the eighth chapter.* Daniel tells us that Gabriel was commanded to make him understand that vision

(8:16). This was not fully done at that interview connected with the vision; he is therefore sent to give Daniel the needed 'skill and understanding,' to explain its 'meaning' by communicating to him the prediction of the seventy weeks."—*Advent Shield*, 1844.

"We claim that the ninth of Daniel is an appendix to the eighth, and that the seventy weeks and the 2300 days or years commence together. *Our opponents deny this.*"—*Signs of the Times*, 1843.

"The grand principle involved in the interpretation of the 2300 days of Daniel 8:14 is that the seventy weeks of Daniel 9, 24 [*sic*], are the first 490 days of the 2300 of the eighth chapter."—*Advent Shield*, p. 49.

"If the connection between the seventy weeks of Daniel 9 and the 2300 days of Daniel 8 does not exist, the whole system is shaken to its foundation; if it does exist, as we suppose, *the system must stand.*"—*Harmony of Prophetic Chronology*, p. 33.

Says the learned Dr. Hales, in commenting upon the seventy weeks, "This chronological prophecy was evidently designed to explain the foregoing vision, especially in its chronological part of the 2300 days."—RH, Feb. 17, 1876.

The Prophetic Chain

Smith in 1854 had carefully shown a link between the seventy weeks and the 2300 days:

It is well known that the main pillar on which rested the proclamation of time, was the great prophetic chain of 2300 days, given to the Prophet, in Daniel 8. In the vision of that chapter, four things were presented to the Prophet: the ram, the he goat, the little horn, and the period of 2300 days. Daniel sought for the meaning of the vision, and Gabriel was commanded to make him understand it. Verses 15, 16. He therefore proceeds to explain the symbols of the ram, he goat and little horn, in plain terms which none could fail to understand; yet, says Daniel, at the end of the chapter, I was astonished at the vision, and none understood it.

There was only one point which the angel had omitted to mention; and that was, Time; hence that was what troubled Daniel, and what none understood. But Gabriel must explain this also; for he had received his commission, Make this man to understand the vision; and he must fulfill it. Therefore he says in chapter 9:22, I am now come forth to give thee skill and understanding. . . . Understand the matter and consider the vision.

He then commences his explanation upon the very point which he omitted in chapter 8; namely, Time. *Seventy weeks*, said the Angel, are determined (literally, *cut off*—Hebraists all admit that the word rendered *determined* signifies *cut off*) upon thy people and upon thy holy city, etc. Verses 25-27. Know therefore and understand that from the going forth of the commandment to restore and build Jerusalem, unto the Messiah the Prince, shall be seven weeks and threescore and two weeks. The street shall be built again, and the wall, even in troublous times. And after threescore and two weeks (from the seven weeks, allowed for the building of Jerusalem) shall Messiah be cut off, but not for himself. . . . And he shall confirm the covenant with many for one week: and in the midst of the week he shall cause the sacrifice and the oblation to cease, etc.

The first question which arises is, Are the seventy weeks a part of the 2300 days? We learn that they are from the following facts:

1. The same person whom Daniel saw at the beginning appears the second time to give him understanding, and refers back to *the* vision, which can be none other than that of chapter 8.

2. He explains the very point which he there omitted; namely, Time.

3. He informs us that seventy weeks are *cut off;* and there is no period given from which they can be taken, but the 2300 days.

Hence it follows that the seventy weeks are the first 490 days of the 2300, and the two periods commence together. The commencement of the seventy weeks, we are told by the Angel, is from the going forth of a commandment to restore and build Jerusalem; therefore that is the starting point for the 2300 days. But when did the commandment go forth? In Ezra 7, we find a commission to him from King Artaxerxes, and a copy of the letter commencing with these words: "Artaxerxes, king of kings, unto Ezra the priest, a scribe of the law of the God of heaven, . . . *I make a decree,*" etc. This decree gave permission to all the people of Israel of their own free will to go up to Jerusalem, and commissioned Ezra to restore the worship of God, and the services of the temple, and to set magistrates and judges who should judge all the people beyond the river, and execute judgment, whether unto death, or to banishment or to confiscation of goods, or to imprisonment. This was in the 7th of Artaxerxes. Verse 8. The 7th of Artaxerxes, as is clearly established, was B.C. 457.—RH, March 21, 1854.

The Decree of Ezra 7

In an article at that same time, James White discussed the decree of Ezra 7 that marks the common beginning of the two time periods by answering someone who said he could not find the "commandment to restore and to build Jerusalem."

Said the angel to Daniel, "Know therefore and understand, that from the going forth of the commandment to restore and to build Jerusalem," etc. Now turn and read the copy of the decree of Artaxerxes "unto Ezra the priest," found in Ezra 7:12-26.

Any impartial reader must see that Jerusalem is restored when the people go back there, re-establish their city polity, and re-commence the regular offering of their sacrifices, and the observance of their daily worship. For this restoration of Jerusalem, the decree made provision when it said: "And thou Ezra, after the wisdom of thy God, that is in thine hand, set magistrates and judges, which may judge all the people that are beyond the river, all such as know the laws of thy God; and teach ye them that know them not. And whosoever will not do the law of thy God, and the law of the king, let judgment be executed speedily upon him, whether it be unto death, or to banishment, or to confiscation of goods, or to imprisonment." Verses 25, 26. Here is the restoration of Jerusalem by the establishment of judges and law.

But did the decree to Ezra also authorize the rebuilding of Jerusalem? It most certainly did. Mark well the unlimited power given to Ezra by this decree. He was empowered, as he understood in his prayer, to proceed at any time with its construction. Here is a quotation from Ezra's prayer, which he offered B.C. 457:

"For we were bond-men; yet our God hath not forsaken us in our bondage, but hath extended mercy unto us in the sight of the kings of Persia, to give us a reviving, to set up the house of our God, and to repair the desolations thereof, AND TO GIVE US A WALL in Judah and Jerusalem." Ezra 9:9.—RH, April 4, 1854.

The First Advent and the 70 Weeks

White then looked in detail at the fulfillment of the seventy-week prophecy in Christ's first advent:

There are distinct bounds at each end of this important prophetic period. Dating its commencement B.C. 457, in the seventh year of Artaxerxes, there is a beautiful harmony with the prophecy of the seventy weeks, and the events which mark their termination.

"Know therefore and understand, that from the going forth of the commandment to restore and to build Jerusalem, unto the Messiah the Prince shall be seven weeks, and threescore and two weeks." Sixty-nine of the seventy weeks reached to the Messiah. Now at what point do we find the Messiah?

Messiah is the "Anointed, the Christ, the Saviour of the world, the Prince of peace." "John seeth Jesus coming unto him, and saith, Behold the Lamb of God which taketh away the sin of the world." Andrew said, "We have found the Messias." Nathaniel said unto Christ, "Rabbi, thou art the Son of God: thou art the King of Israel." The woman at Jacob's well said, "I know that Messias cometh, which is called Christ; when he is come he will tell us all things. Jesus saith unto her, I that speak unto thee am he." And many of the Samaritans said, We "know that this is indeed the Christ, the Saviour of the world." "Peter said, Thou art the Christ, the Son of the living God. Jesus said, Flesh and blood hath not revealed it unto thee, but my Father which is in heaven." At Christ's baptism the Holy Ghost descended in a bodily shape like a dove upon Him; and a voice from heaven, and testified, saying, "Thou art my beloved Son; in thee I am well pleased."

All this and much more might be added to this clear testimony, that the Messiah was manifested at the commencement of His ministry. This settles the termination of the 69 weeks. After Jesus was baptized, He preached, saying, "The time is fulfilled." (Accomplished—Campbell.) Mark 1:15. What time? No time can be found to be fulfilled, but the 69 weeks, which are accomplished at "the Messiah the Prince," when He was baptized. This, according to Usher, was A.D. 26. Here is fixed the termination of the 69 weeks.—Ibid.

Next White turned his attention to the last, or seventieth week, and its events:

> "And after threescore and two weeks [from the end of seven weeks, allowed to build Jerusalem] shall Messiah be cut off, but not for himself." Dan. 9:26. How long after 69 weeks, or Christ's baptism, before Messiah was cut off, or crucified? This may easily be determined, by ascertaining the length of Christ's ministry, from His baptism to His cross where He was cut off. This may be determined by the number of yearly passovers He attended. We find that but four passovers occurred during His ministry, which He attended [John 2:13; 5:1; 6:4; 13:1]; and at the fourth He was crucified. These four passovers could not cover more than three and a half years. Those three and a half years added to Usher's chronology of Christ's baptism, A.D. 26-27, could not extend beyond A.D. 31; where must stand the cross.
>
> Clear it is, that as at His baptism the 69 weeks ended, so at His cross, the end of the three and a half years more, must be the midst of the week where Christ caused the sacrifice and oblation to cease by becoming our passover, sacrificed for us.—*Ibid.*

But what about the remaining three and a half years? White continued:

> The cross plainly stands according to the Scriptures, in the midst [middle] of the one week, the seventieth, during which He was to confirm the covenant with many. Dan. 9:27. This fact shows that the apostles had but half of one week, three and a half years, left them in which to confirm the covenant. Now as the cross stood in the Spring, A.D. 31, the middle of the seventieth week, three and a half years more, the confirming, by them that heard Him [Heb. 2:3], must bring us to the Autumn of A.D. 34, where ended the seventy weeks, or 490 years of the 2300 [Dan. 8:14], which leaves 1810 years to transpire after the Fall of A.D. 34, which ended A.D. 1844.—*Ibid.*

Is the Decree of Ezra 7 the Correct One?

In an article titled "The 2300 Days, What Takes Place When They Terminate?" Uriah Smith dealt with the confusion that existed for years after the Disappointment among those who continued to believe that Christ was to return at the end of the 2300 days. Some advanced a decree in the twentieth year of Artaxerxes as the beginning of the time prophecy. That would bring the end date to 1857. Smith wrote his article in *that year*. Of the 2300-day prophecy, he said, "Every year has been more or less prolific of new points set for its termination. As point after point has passed, the matter has been extenuated and extenuated, upon every imaginable ground that human ingenuity could invent, till now the most distant point, the present year, to which it can possibly extend, has been reached,

69

and we wait to see, when this is past, where their landing point will be."—RH, May 7, 1857.

Setting New Times

He noted the effect of repeatedly setting new times for the second coming of Christ:

> Point after point, as we have said, has been set, and passed; but their advocates, nothing daunted by their passing, which shows again that they put no great faith in their own teaching, have been ready to gad about and set another. To such an extent has this been carried that we can look upon it in no other light than mere trifling with the prophetic scriptures. Against such a course we enter our solemn protest. What is, what must be, its effect upon the community at large? Most disastrous! The Advent movement in the eyes of the people is turned into a mere farce!—*Ibid.*

Smith asked:

> What are we to expect at the end of the prophetic period of the 2300 days? Is it said that the Lord shall then come? We answer, No. But it is said, The prophecy reads that then the Sanctuary shall be cleansed. Very well, we believe it; but wherein does this prove that the Lord will then appear the second time? It is answered, The earth is the Sanctuary, it is to be cleansed by fire, and this takes place at the coming of Christ. To these assertions we object.
>
> The earth, we know, is to be purified by fire, but when does this take place? Peter tells us [2 Peter 3:7] that it is reserved unto fire against the day of judgment and perdition of ungodly men. When does the perdition of ungodly men come? Answer: At the second resurrection, 1000 years from the first. Rev. 20. We aver therefore that the renovation of the earth by fire will not take place at the second coming of Christ, but 1000 years after; and hence it has no connection with the 2300 days.—*Ibid.*

Finally, he closed with an appeal to those who would continue to set new dates for Christ to return:

> We have heretofore called upon that class of Advent believers called Timeists, for their evidence that the Lord would appear at the end of the 2300 days. We have not seen it presented. Again we put the question, What do you expect to transpire when the days end? The Lord will not then come: there is no such promise. But another work entirely is there located; namely, then shall the Sanctuary be cleansed. And, we repeat, could it be shown that the period extends to the present year, you are doomed to disappointment, if you embrace in your expectations the coming of the Lord.—*Ibid.*

The Meaning of Chathak—Determined or Cut Off?

In his extended series on the sanctuary in 1876, Smith called ten witnesses to the interpretation of "determined" as "cut off." They were largely non-Millerite scholars:

First witness. " 'Seventy weeks are *determined,*' literally *'cut off.'* Hebraists all admit that the word determined, in our English version, does signify *'cut off.' Not one* has disputed it."—Josiah Litch, *Midnight Cry,* vol. 4, No. 25.

Second witness. "Seventy weeks have been cut off upon thy people and upon thy holy city, to finish the transgression, and to make an end of sin offerings, and to make atonement for iniquity, and to bring in everlasting righteousness, and to seal the vision and prophecy, and to anoint the Most Holy." Dan. 9:24.—*Whiting's Translation.*

Third witness. Gesenius, the standard Hebrew lexicographer, thus defines this word in his Hebrew lexicon: *"Nechtak:* Properly, to cut off; tropically, to divide, and so to determine, to decree."

Fourth witness. The Chaldeo-Rabbinic Dictionary of Stocius, defines the word *nechtak* as follows: *"Scidit, abscidit, conscidit, incidit, excidit*—to cut, to cut away, to cut in pieces, to cut or engrave, to cut off."

Fifth witness. Mercerus, in his "Thesaurus," furnishes a specimen of Rabbinical usage in the phrase *chatikan shel basar,* "a piece of flesh," or "a cut of flesh." He translates the word as it occurs in Daniel 9:24, by *"praecisa est,"* was cut off.

Sixth witness. Arias Montanus in a literal version of the text translates it *"decisa est,"* was cut off; in the marginal reading, which is grammatically correct, the rendering is in the plural, *"decisae sunt,"* were cut off.

Seventh witness. In the Latin version of Junius and Tremellius, *nechtak* (the passive of *chathak)* is rendered *"decisae sunt,"* were cut off.

Eighth witness. Theodotion's Greek version of Daniel (which is the version used in the Vatican copy of the Septuagint, as being the most faithful), renders it by συνετμηθησαν, "were cut off;" and the Venetian copy by τετμηνται, "have been cut."

Ninth witness. In the Vulgate the phrase is *"abbreviatae sunt,"* have been shortened.

"Thus Chaldaic and Rabbinical authority, and that of the earliest versions, the Septuagint and Vulgate, give the single signification of *cutting off* to this verb."

Tenth witness. Hengstenberg, who enters into a critical examination of the text, says: "But the very use of the word, which does not elsewhere occur, while others, much more frequently used, were at hand if Daniel had wished to express the idea of determination, and of which he has elsewhere, and even in this portion availed himself, seems to argue that the word stands from regard to its original meaning, and represents the seventy weeks in contrast with a determination of time *(en platei)* as a period cut off from subsequent duration, and accurately limited."—*Christology of the Old Testament,* vol. 2, p. 301. Washington, 1839.—RH, Feb. 17, 1876.

Smith concluded:

71

Beyond question the seventy weeks are cut off from some other period; and just as evidently that other period is the 2300 days of chapter 8. Should it be asked why our translators render the word "determined" when it so obviously signifies "cut off," a sufficient answer would be that they doubtless overlooked the connection between the eighth and ninth chapters; and, considering it improper to speak of a period of time as cut off, when nothing was given from which it could be cut off, they gave the word its tropical instead of its literal meaning.—*Ibid.*

Three Confessions

J. N. Andrews gave full support to the relationship between the seventy weeks and the 2300 days by considering three "confessions" regarding the disappointment of 1844:

That a confession of error should be made by all who then proclaimed the coming of the Lord, we think no one disposed to deny. Thus far we stand on common ground with all who profess the Advent faith. Now we ask why it was that those who then expected the Saviour were disappointed? It is at this point that a difference of opinion begins. Three answers have been returned:

1. Because the 70 weeks are not a part of the 2300 days.
2. Because that the 70 weeks were not then dated from the true decree.
3. Because that the earth is not the Sanctuary.

Here are three confessions of error. Which one of them shall be adopted as the proper confession? Those who make the first of these confessions acknowledge that the evidence sustaining the original date of the 70 weeks, *viz.*, B.C. 457, is not capable of being set aside; and that if the 70 weeks are the first 490 days of the 2300, "it is as clear that the 2300 days ended in the Autumn of 1844, as it is that the sun arose this morning."

But if the 2300 days ended in 1844 it is demonstrated that no part of the earth is the Sanctuary, for as yet, no part of the earth is cleansed. It follows, therefore, that those who make the first of these confessions, *viz.*, the denial that the 70 weeks are a part of the 2300 days, do it because they are not willing to yield the view that the earth or a part of it is the Sanctuary.—RH, Oct. 30, 1855.

He followed with a look at the second "confession":

But how is it with those who make the second confession? They do not deny that the 70 weeks are a part of the 2300 days. They acknowledge that Gabriel in Daniel 9 completed the charge given him in Daniel 8:16, which was to make Daniel understand the vision; which according to verse 27, he did not accomplish in chapter 8. . . .

They admit that the 70 weeks which were "cut off" form the first 490 days of the long period in "the vision" which Gabriel was explaining: and that the remainder of the 2300 days extend 1810 days from the termination of the 70 weeks. But as the earth was not burned in 1844, they move the date of the 70 weeks forward thirteen years to the twentieth of Artaxerxes, thus moving forward thirteen years, the date of the commencement of Christ's ministry, and of His crucifixion, and of the commencement of the gospel to the Gentiles.—*Ibid.*

Andrews then drew some conclusions:

It is apparent, therefore, that those who deny the connection between the 70 weeks and the 2300 days, and those who attempt to set the 70 weeks forward thirteen years, have each the same article of faith to which they tenaciously cling, which is the grand cause of each of these important errors. It is this doctrine that causes all the trouble, *viz.*, that the earth is the Sanctuary, and that the cleansing of the Sanctuary is effected by the second coming of Christ. What mighty array of evidence, then, can be adduced to prove that the earth, or a part of the earth, is the Sanctuary, that men should be willing to yield almost anything else rather than acknowledge that in this they may have been mistaken? In examining the third confession we shall see.—*Ibid.*

The third "perspective" Andrews stated quite simply:

The third confession is an acknowledgment that the Advent people were mistaken when they said that the earth was the Sanctuary, and that Christ must come and burn the earth in order to cleanse the Sanctuary.—*Ibid.*

Now Andrews clearly identified himself and the Seventh-day Adventist Church with those who make the third declaration:

But what are the reasons which sustain those who make the third confession?

1. They are unable to deny the connection of the 70 weeks and 2300 days, or to set the 70 weeks forward thirteen years. To do this would be to deny the plainest evidence.

2. But they confess that the earth is not the Sanctuary, because that the Bible never calls it by that name. The word is used in the Bible 146 times, but it is never applied to the earth.

3. The Old Testament, by a hundred plain testimonies, designates the *tabernacle* of the Lord as His Sanctuary. Even the two or three texts that are supposed to teach that some part of the earth is the Sanctuary are readily reconciled with this cloud of witnesses.

4. The New Testament tells us that there are two covenants, and names with distinctness the Sanctuary of each. This covers all the ground and settles the Sanctuary question beyond all controversy. The Sanctuary of the first covenant was the tabernacle which Moses erected as a pattern of the true tabernacle. Heb. 9:1-5. "Then verily the first covenant had also ordinances of divine service, and a worldly sanctuary. For there was a tabernacle made, the first, wherein was the candlestick, and the table, and the shew-bread; which is called the

Sanctuary. And after the second veil, the tabernacle, which is called the Holiest of all: which had the golden censer, and the ark of the covenant overlaid round about with gold, wherein was the golden pot that had manna, and Aaron's rod that budded, and the tables of the covenant; and over it the cherubims of glory shadowing the mercy seat; of which we cannot now speak particularly." The Sanctuary of the better covenant is the true tabernacle itself, which the Lord pitched and not man, of which Moses erected a copy. Heb. 8:1-6.—*Ibid.*

In conclusion Andrews connected the Old Testament sanctuary with its pattern in heaven, pointed out in Daniel 8:14:

The sixteenth of Leviticus plainly teaches that the Sanctuary of the first covenant was cleansed by blood at the conclusion of the yearly round of services, because the sins of the people had been borne there. The ninth of Hebrews teaches that the new covenant Sanctuary must be cleansed for the same reason, but with better sacrifices than the former. Verses 22-24. "And almost all things are by the law purged with blood; and without shedding of blood is no remission. It was therefore necessary that the patterns of things in the heavens should be purified with these; but the heavenly things themselves with better sacrifices than these. For Christ is not entered into the holy places made with hands, which are the figures of the true; but into heaven itself, now to appear in the presence of God for us."

If these plain testimonies are allowed, they settle the question that the earth is not the Sanctuary; that the Sanctuary is the tabernacle of the Lord; and that the tabernacle is cleansed with blood and not with fire; and that the work of cleansing the sanctuary is the conclusion of the work of the High Priest before leaving the tabernacle of God. Consequently the cleansing of the Sanctuary precedes the revelation of our great High Priest.

This is the third confession. Is it not as fair and honorable a confession as the first or the second? It is not a confession that the 70 weeks are not a part of the 2300 days, or that the 70 weeks should be set forward thirteen years. Overwhelming evidence forbids such a confession. But it is a frank acknowledgment of erroneous views respecting the Sanctuary. In making this confession we do not reject the smallest portion of divine testimony, but on the contrary a multitude of testimonies constrain us thus to confess.—*Ibid.*

Precedent for Disappointment

At about the same time, Uriah Smith acknowledged the criticism of the Millerite movement and the Disappointment. He turned to a familiar Bible experience as a precedent:

It may now be said, You admit that your expectations in then looking for the Lord were wrong; why then do you not reject a movement which was the result of those expectations? Here, for our encouragement and comfort, our past experience and disappointment are not without a precedent in the history of God's people. Go back with me to the time of Christ's entry into Jerusalem, and explain the meaning of that shouting multitude. Why are all classes, young and old, pressing in the way before and behind Him, and, absorbed in one emotion, shouting, Hosanna to the Son of David! Blessed be the King that cometh in the name of the Lord! Hosanna in the highest!

They cut down branches from the trees and strewed them in the way, and they spread their garments before Him, an act which was done to royalty only. Doubtless they expected that His kingdom should then be set up. In their rejoicing they quote from a psalm which probably applies to the future reign and triumph of the Messiah. They thought the time had come for those events to be realized. In these expectations they were to be disappointed; but were they therefore wrong in shouting and rejoicing as they did? Let Jesus answer: "I tell you that if these should hold their peace, the stones would immediately cry out."—RH, Sept. 18, 1855.

Why the Disappointment?

James White saw the same reason for the Disappointment:

Our disappointment did not arise from mistaking the manner and object of the second advent, for no truth is more distinctly stated in the sacred Scriptures than the personal and visible second appearing of Jesus Christ to raise the righteous dead, change to immortality the living righteous, and to destroy the unbelieving world.

Nor did our disappointment arise from misapplying the prophetic symbols of Daniel and John. A careful review of the subject confirms us that the application of these symbols made by the Adventists of 1840-44 was correct.

Nor did our disappointment arise from a misapplication of the prophetic periods. The year-day theory is well sustained. The argument by which the original date of the seventy weeks of the ninth chapter of Daniel is sustained is invulnerable. And Adventists correctly held that the seventy weeks were a part of the 2300 days. These two points relative to the seventy weeks being correct, we had sufficient reasons for believing that the 2300 days would terminate in the year 1844.

Neither did our disappointment arise from believing that at the end of the 2300 days the work of cleansing the sanctuary would take place. For it is plainly stated, "Unto two thousand and three hundred days; then shall the sanctuary be cleansed." Dan. 8:14.

But when we said that this earth, or a part of this earth, was the sanctuary, and that Christ must descend from Heaven at the end of the 2300 days, to purify the earth by fire, we looked for that which the Bible did not warrant us to expect. Here was the cause of our disappointment.—RH, April 5, 1870.

Artaxerxes' Decree and the Seventy Weeks

In an article composed just before he went to Europe as the first official Seventh-day Adventist missionary, Andrews spoke of the sequence of events leading up to the decree of Artaxerxes in 457 B.C.:

> "Know therefore," said Gabriel, "and understand that from the going forth of the commandment to restore and to build Jerusalem unto the Messiah the Prince shall be seven weeks and threescore and two weeks." Dan. 9:25. The commandment for the restoration of Jerusalem, which city then lay in ruins, is the event which marks the commencement of this period. Cyrus gave the Jews permission to return and build a temple, but did not say anything respecting the city itself. Ezra 1. This decree Darius renewed when the Jews were hindered by their enemies, and he provided means for the expense of finishing the temple. Ezra 6.
>
> But Artaxerxes added to the work of Cyrus and Darius the full restoration of the city to its ancient privileges, and the re-establishment of the law of God as the law of the city; and he authorized the rebuilding of its walls. Ezra 7:11-26; 9:9. The commandment is the prophetic commandment of the God of Heaven (Isa. 44:26-28; 45:13), and was carried into effect by Cyrus, Darius, and Artaxerxes, whose successive action is recognized as the legal establishment of that commandment by the authority of the Persian Empire. Ezra 6:14.
>
> The decree of Artaxerxes, which marks the going forth of the commandment, was in the year B.C. 457 (see margin of Ezra 7), a date which has been established by the infallible testimony of many eclipses. Sixty-nine weeks, or 483 prophetic days, extend from this date to the Messiah, that is, to Christ. This period was fulfilled in exactly 483 years, which proves that we have made no mistake in reckoning Daniel's days as years, nor in fixing their date at B.C. 457.—RH, March 10, 1874.

Jesus Comes on Time

The pioneers repeatedly stressed the importance of Christ's first advent to the earth as evidence for the accuracy of the 2300-day prophecy. Andrews said:

> It was in the fall of A.D. 27, just 483 full years from the going forth of the commandment in B.C. 457, that our Lord began His ministry. And this was the announcement which He made: "The Time Is Fulfilled." Mark 1:15. He did in these words refer to the sixty-nine weeks which marked the commencement of His ministry, and He announced the fulfillment of that period. For the period extends not simply to the birth of the Saviour, but to His anointing, which took place at His baptism, the word Messiah signifying the anointed one. See John 1:41; Acts 10:40, 41; Luke 3:21, 22; 4:14-21.
>
> The sixty-nine weeks did, therefore, end with the beginning of our Lord's ministry in the fall of A.D. 27. One week of the seventy remained in which the covenant was to be confirmed with many. Verse 27. In the midst of this week, the sacrifice and oblation were to cease. This must signify that He should take these away by becoming Himself the great sacrifice for sin which these typified. Heb. 10:1-13; Col. 2:14-17.

And so it was that our Lord preached during three years and a half until the spring of A.D. 31, when He was crucified for the sins of men. This date, Dr. Hales, one of the most distinguished of chronologists, establishes by conclusive evidence. See his *Analysis of Chronology*, second edition, vol. 1, pp. 94-100.

There remained of the period which was specially assigned to the Jews three and a half prophetic days to complete the seventy weeks. The termination of this period in A.D. 34 marked the close of the exclusive work for the Jews, and the commencement of the work for the Gentiles in the conversion of Saul, who was at once commissioned to them. Acts 26:15-17. Here ended the seventy weeks which were cut off from the 2300 days. When these 490 days were finished, there remained 1810 days before the time should come for the cleansing of the sanctuary. As the 490 ended in the fall of A.D. 34, the remaining 1810 days ended in the fall of 1844.—*Ibid.*

Once again Andrews recalled the work of William Miller:

In the great Advent movement under the preaching of William Miller and his fellow-laborers, the evidence was brought out with great clearness that the 2300 days would end in 1844. He believed that the sanctuary to be cleansed is our earth. He found no testimony in the Bible that the earth is the sanctuary, but he did find that the earth is to be purified by fire (2 Peter 3:7-13), and so he inferred that this was the sanctuary which Michael said should be cleansed at the end of the 2300 days. He therefore concluded that this period was given to mark the time of Christ's coming. And as it was sufficiently evident from the several great lines of prophecy in Daniel and Revelation, and from the signs of the times, that the advent of Christ was at the doors, the time was preached in connection with the signs with very great solemnity and power.—*Ibid.*

In Conclusion

From the very first, the pioneers recognized a connection between the seventy weeks and the 2300 days. As they compared and blended Daniel 8 and 9, they came to several clear conclusions:

1. The seventy weeks and 2300 days are *one* prophecy. They began at the same date, and are clearly linked together.

2. *Chathak*, translated as "determined" in the King James Version of Scripture, meant "cut off." The seventy weeks were sliced off at the beginning from the 2300 days.

3. The pioneers recognized much evidence substantiating the 457 B.C. date for starting the prophetic time period. Today we have an even greater amount.

4. And they perceived as the real reason Sunday-observing Adventists wished either to shift the date or to separate the two time periods was that they wanted to dissociate the prophecy from

heaven's sanctuary.

Confident in the knowledge of careful and prayerful Bible study, and with the remarkable confirming visions of Ellen White, they boldly championed what they believed. They were confident that God had led them to the truth about what had happened in 1844.

* * * *

Ellen White spoke quite directly on the seventy weeks and 2300 days in the following references:

Seventy weeks
The Desire of Ages, pp. 233-235; *The Great Controversy*, pp. 323-329, 345-347, 410; *Prophets and Kings*, pp. 698, 699; *The Sanctified Life*, pp. 48, 49.

Began in 457 B.C.
The Desire of Ages, p. 233; *The Great Controversy*, pp. 326-328, 410; *Prophets and Kings*, pp. 698, 699.

Ended in A.D. 34.
The Desire of Ages, p. 233; *The Great Controversy*, pp. 327, 328, 410; *Prophets and Kings*, p. 699.

2300 Days
Early Writings, pp. 42, 43, 86, 253; *The Great Controversy*, pp. 429, 430, 435.

Began in 457 B.C.
The Desire of Ages, p. 233; *The Great Controversy*, pp. 326-328, 398, 399, 410; *Prophets and Kings*, pp. 698, 699.

Ended in 1844
Early Writings, pp. 236, 237, 243, 246, 251, 253; *The Great Controversy*, pp. 417, 421, 422, 429, 480, 486; *The Story of Redemption*, pp. 377, 378; *Testimonies*, vol. 1, p. 58.

* * * *

ARTICLES QUOTED IN THIS CHAPTER

James White
Dec. 6, 1853, The 2300 Days
April 4, 1854, The Seventy Weeks
April 5, 1870, Our Faith and Hope—Our Disappointment (Series)

J. N. Andrews
Dec. 23, 1852, The Sanctuary
Oct. 30, 1855, The Sanctuary and Its Cleansing
March 10, 1874, The Sanctuary of the Bible

Uriah Smith
March 21, 1854, The Sanctuary
Sept. 18, 1855, The Original Advent Faith
May 7, 1857, The 2300 Days. What Takes Place When They Terminate?
Feb. 17, 1876, The Sanctuary (Series)

6

The Little Horn

From the beginning of the movement that was to become the Seventh-day Adventist Church, opponents to its position on the 2300 days have attempted to connect the period with the Syrian king Antiochus Epiphanes. Such an interpretation actually antedated the rise of Seventh-day Adventism by hundreds of years. The eighth of twenty-six kings who successively ruled a portion of the old Greek empire, he has sometimes been called the little horn of Daniel 8:9. The theory equates a period of oppression by him with a literal time fulfillment of the 2300-day prophecy. J. N. Andrews looked carefully at the evidence for applying the symbol to Antiochus instead of papal Rome. He began his discussion by quoting Daniel 8:

> "And in the latter time of their kingdom, when the transgressors are come to the full, a king of fierce countenance, and understanding dark sentences, shall stand up. And his power shall be mighty, but not by his own power; and he shall destroy wonderfully, and shall prosper, and practice, and shall destroy the mighty and the holy people. And through his policy, also, he shall cause craft to prosper in his hand; he shall also stand up against the Prince of princes; but he shall be broken without hand." Verses 23-25.
>
> To avoid the application of this prophecy to the Roman power, Pagan and Papal, the Papists have shifted it from Rome to Antiochus Ephiphanes, a Syrian king who *could not resist* the mandates of Rome. See notes of the Douay [Romish] Bible on Daniel 7; 8; 11. This application is made by the Papists, to save their church from any share in the fulfillment of the prophecy; and in this, they have been followed by the mass of opposers to Advent faith.—RH, Dec. 23, 1852.

Not Antiochus

Andrews systematically examined several lines of evidence that the little horn was *not* Antiochus:

1. The four kingdoms into which the dominion of Alexander was divided are symbolized by the four horns of the goat. Now this Antiochus was but one of the twenty-five kings* that constituted the Syrian horn. How, then, could he, at the *same time*, be *another* remarkable horn?

2. The ram, according to this vision, became great; the goat waxed very great; but the little horn became exceeding great. How absurd and ludicrous is the following application of this comparison:

Great	Very Great	Exceeding Great
PERSIA	GRECIA	ANTIOCHUS

How easy and natural is the following:

Great	Very Great	Exceeding Great
PERSIA	GRECIA	ROME

3. The Medo-Persian empire is simply called GREAT. Verse 4. The Bible informs us that it extended "from India even unto Ethiopia, over an hundred seven and twenty provinces." Esther 1:1. This was succeeded by the Grecian power, which is called VERY GREAT. Verse 8. Then comes the power in question which is called EXCEEDING GREAT. Verse 9. Was Antiochus exceeding great when compared with Alexander, the conqueror of the world? Let an item from the *Encyclopedia of Religious Knowledge* answer:
"Finding his resources exhausted, he resolved to go into Persia, to levy tributes and collect large sums which he had *agreed to pay to the Romans.*"
Surely we need not question which was exceeding great, the Roman power which exacted the tribute, or Antiochus who was *compelled* to pay it.

4. The power in question was "little" at first, but it waxed or grew "exceeding great toward the south, and toward the east, and toward the pleasant land." What can this describe but the conquering marches of a mighty power? Rome was almost directly northwest from Jerusalem, and its conquests in Asia and Africa were, of course, toward the east and south; but where were Antiochus' conquests? He came into possession of a kingdom already established, and Sir Isaac Newton says, "He did *not* enlarge it."

5. Out of many reasons that might be added to the above we name but one. This power was to stand up against the Prince of princes. Verse 25. The Prince of princes is Jesus Christ. Rev. 1:5; 17:14; 19:16. But

---

* Some commentators suggest a total of twenty-six kings.

Antiochus died 164 years before our Lord was born. It is settled, therefore, that another power is the subject of this prophecy.—*Ibid.*

Rome Is the Little Horn

After expressing what he believed the little horn was *not*, Andrews offered arguments that demonstrated to him that the horn symbolized Rome:

1. This power was to come forth from one of the four kingdoms of Alexander's empire. Let us remember that nations are not brought into prophecy till somehow connected with the people of God. Rome had been in existence many years before it was noticed in prophecy; and Rome had made Macedon, one of the four horns of the Grecian goat, a part of itself B.C. 168, about ten years before its first connection with the people of God. See 1 Mac. 8. So that Rome could as truly be said to be "out of one of them," as the *ten horns* of the fourth beast in the seventh chapter, could be said to come *out of that* beast, when they were ten kingdoms set up by the conquerors of Rome.

2. It was to wax exceeding great toward the south, and toward the east, and toward the pleasant land. [Palestine. Ps. 106:24; Zech. 7:14.] This was true of Rome in every particular. Witness its conquests in Africa and Asia, and its overthrow of the place and nation of the Jews. John 11:48.

3. It was to cast down of the host and of the stars. This is predicted respecting the dragon. Rev. 12:3, 4. All admit that the dragon was Rome. Who can fail to see their identity?

4. Rome was emphatically a king of fierce countenance, and one that did understand dark sentences. Moses used similar language, when as all agree, he predicted the Roman power. Deut. 28:49, 50.

5. Rome did destroy wonderfully. Witness its overthrow of all opposing powers.

6. Rome has destroyed more of "the mighty and the holy people" than all other persecuting powers combined. From fifty to one hundred millions of the church have been slain by it.

7. Rome did stand up against the Prince of princes. The Roman power nailed Jesus Christ to the cross. Acts 4:26, 27; Matt. 27:2; Rev. 12:4.

8. This power is to "be broken without hand." How clear the reference to the stone "cut out without hand" that smote the image. Dan. 2:34. Its destruction then does not take place until the final overthrow of earthly power. These facts are conclusive proof that Rome is the subject of this prophecy.—*Ibid.*

Paganism, the Papacy, and the Sanctuary

The pioneers did not ignore or deny the context of Daniel 8:13, 14. In fact, they worked with it, seeing paganism removed by the Papacy. They recognized that God's sanctuary and His church (host) were "trodden under foot" (persecuted) by both powers. J. N.

THE SANCTUARY, 1844, AND THE PIONEERS

Andrews drew attention to William Miller's exposition under the heading "The Two Desolations Are Paganism and Papacy":

"I . . . could find no other case in which it [the daily] was found, but in Daniel. I then [by the aid of a concordance] took those words which stood in connection with it, 'take away;' he shall *take away* the daily; 'from the time the daily shall be *taken away*' etc. I read on, and thought I should find no light on the text; finally I came to 2 Thess. 2:7, 8. 'For the mystery of iniquity doth already work; only he who now letteth will let, until he be *taken out of the way*, and then shall that wicked be revealed,' etc.

"And when I had come to that text, O, how clear and glorious the truth appeared! There it is ! That is the daily! Well, now, what does Paul mean by 'he who now letteth' or hindereth? By 'the man of sin,' and the 'wicked,' Popery is meant. Well, what is it which hinders Popery from being revealed? Why, it is Paganism; well, then, 'the daily' must mean Paganism.—[William Miller, in] *Second Advent Manual*, p. 66, quoted in RH, Jan. 6, 1853.

Andrews agreed with Miller's reasoning:

It needs no argument to prove that the two grand forms of opposition, by which Satan has desolated the church, and trod under foot the sanctuary of the living God, are none other than Paganism and Popery. It is also a clear point that the change from one of these desolations to the other did occur under the Roman power.

Paganism, from the days of the kings of Assyria down to the period when it became so far modified that it took the name of Popery, had been the daily [or, as Prof. Whiting renders it, "the continual"] desolation, by which Satan had stood up against the cause of Jehovah.—*Ibid.*

He then continued:

The language of Paul is to the point: "For the mystery of iniquity [Popery] *doth already work*; only he who now letteth will let, until he be taken out of the way. And then shall that Wicked be revealed, whom the Lord shall consume with the Spirit of his mouth, and shall destroy with the brightness of his coming." 2 Thess. 2:7, 8. That Paul refers to Paganism and Popery none question.—And here is direct proof that Popery, the abomination of desolation, had in Paul's day, already begun to work.

Nor was it a very great change of character when Satan transformed his counterfeit worship from Paganism to Popery. The same temples, altars, incense, priests and worshipers were ready, with little change, to serve as the appendages of the Papal abomination. The statue of Jupiter readily changed to that of Peter, the prince of the apostles; and the Pantheon, which had been the temple of all the gods, without difficulty became the sanctuary of all the saints.—*Ibid.*

THE LITTLE HORN

More Evidence on the Little Horn

Reasoning further, Andrews said:

The change from Paganism to Popery is clearly shown in John's view of the transfer of power from the dragon of Revelation 12 to the beast of Revelation 13.—And that they are essentially the same thing is evident from the fact that both the dragon and the beast are represented with *the* seven heads; thus showing that, in a certain sense, either may be understood to cover the whole time. And in the same sense we understand that either abomination covers all the period.—Christ's reference to the abomination of desolation [Matt. 24:15; Luke 21:20] is an absolute demonstration that Rome is the Little Horn of Daniel 8:9-14.—*Ibid.*

The Sanctuary "Trodden Under Foot"

A month later in the same series of articles, Andrews had more to say on Daniel 8:13 and the role of the little horn in treading down the sanctuary. "The agents by which the sanctuary is trodden under foot are the daily, or continual desolation, and the transgression, or abomination of desolation. Dan. 8:13; 11:31; 12:11. These two desolations, as we have already seen, are Paganism and Papacy."—RH, Feb. 3, 1853.

He agreed with Uriah Smith that it is possible for heaven's sanctuary to be "trodden under foot." "The New Testament shows us that wicked men (apostates) tread under foot the minister of the heavenly sanctuary, our Lord Jesus Christ. Heb. 10:29; 8:1, 2. If they can tread under foot the minister of that sanctuary, then they can tread under foot the sanctuary itself. It is not impossible that the Pagan and Papal desolations should be represented as treading under foot the heavenly sanctuary, when the same vision represents the little horn as stamping upon the stars. Dan. 8:10. And when it is expressly predicted that the Papal power should war against the tabernacle of God in heaven. Rev. 13:5-7."—*Ibid.*

In Conclusion

It is evident, from the record, that the pioneers did not ignore the context of Daniel 8:13, 14. They saw the prophecy fulfilled in paganism being absorbed by the Papacy. Despite efforts by several commentators to identify the little horn of Daniel 8 with other powers in history, Seventh-day Adventists have persistently applied the symbol to Rome.

* * * * *

Ellen White has applied the fulfillment of the little horn

prophecy to Rome in the following references:
The Great Controversy, pp. 439, 446.

* * * *

ARTICLES QUOTED IN THIS CHAPTER

J. N. Andrews
Dec. 23, 1852, The Sanctuary (Series)
Jan. 6, 1853, The Sanctuary
Feb. 3, 1853, The Sanctuary

7

The Investigative Judgment

While the term "investigative judgment" did not come into immediate use among pioneer Adventists, we do find frequent references to judgment from the very beginning. For example, J. N. Loughborough remembered J. V. Himes's words of 1844:

> "We told the ministers and churches that it was no part of our business to break them up, or to divide and distract them. We had one distinct object: that was to give the cry, the warning of 'the judgment at the door.' "—Quoted in RH, Nov. 19, 1857.

He also recalled a statement in the *Advent Shield* (vol. 1, no. 1, p. 86):*

> "We look upon the proclamation which has been made (this was just after the time expired) as being the cry of the angel who proclaimed, 'The hour of his judgment is come.' " Revelation 14:6, 7.—*Ibid.*

During the time that Crosier was working on the concept of the cleansing of the sanctuary for the *Day-Star*, William Miller wrote a letter (March 20, 1845) that the same publication also printed. In it Miller applied the concept of judgment to the closing ministry of Christ in the heavenly sanctuary:

> "That the prophetic numbers did close in 1844, I can have but little doubt. What then was there worthy of note that could be said to answer to the ending of the periods under these numbers so emphatically describing the end? I answer. The first thing I will notice is, "The hour of his Judgment is come." I ask, is there anything in the

---

* The *Advent Shield,* launched after the spring Disappointment in 1844 to review evidence of God's leadership in the Millerite movement to that point, was a forerunner of the *Advent Review.*

Scriptures to show that the hour has not come, or in our present position to show, that God is not now in His last Judicial character deciding the cases of all the righteous, so that Christ (speaking after the manner of men) will know whom to collect at His coming, or the angels may know whom to gather, when they are sent to gather together the elect, whom God has in this hour of His judgment justified? Rom. 8:33. . . . It also seems by John's description of this event, Rev. 19:1, 2, 11, that the scene of the judgment begins in heaven, and the first thing mortals on earth will see will be the messenger of God, Rev. 20:1, who is Jesus Christ, descending from God, to execute the judgment written in heaven, and fulfill the decrees and promises made in heaven by Him who sitteth on the great white throne. . . . If this is true, who can say God is not already justifying His Sanctuary, and will yet justify us in preaching the time?"—*Day-Star*, April 8, 1845, quoted in *SDA Encyclopedia*, p. 670.

J. N. Andrews later cited the words of Sylvester Bliss in the *Advent Shield* in 1845:

"We are inclined to the opinion that the judgment is after death and before the resurrection; and that before that event the acts of all men will be adjudicated; so that the resurrection of the righteous is their full acquittal and redemption—their sins being blotted out when the times of refreshing shall have come (Acts 8:19); while the fact that the wicked are not raised [for 1,000 years] proves that they were previously condemned."—RH, Feb. 8, 1870.

Also Andrews quoted Josiah Litch in his *Prophetic Expositions* (1842): "No human tribunal would think of executing judgment on a prisoner until after his trial; much less will God. He will bring every work into judgment, with every secret thing, whether it be good or evil."—*Ibid.*

David Arnold, writing in *The Present Truth*, December, 1849, seven times spoke of the High Priest going into the Most Holy Place wearing "the breast-plate of judgment" as mentioned in Exodus 28:28-30, a concept applied to Christ's ministry in heaven.

Joseph Bates also mentioned the "breast-plate of judgment" on the High Priest when he wrote that "the precious promise of the Bridegroom to all such is 'Because thou hast kept *the word of my patience*, I ALSO WILL KEEP THEE,' etc. Amen. This is the state of the Israel of God, and must be until the house of God is judged, 1 Peter 4:17, and fitted for deliverance."—RH, December, 1850.*

J. N. Loughborough, in 1854, proclaimed that "the first angel's message is a definite one. Take the definiteness from it, and it would herald no new idea, but would only be 'Fear God, . . . for the

---

* Both Joseph Bates and O. R. L. Crosier adopted the breastplate concept from Turner and Jacobs, Millerite Adventists.

judgment is coming.' Neither Luther, Wesley, or any of the reformers gave a definite proclamation in regard to the judgment. Said Martin Luther, 'The judgment is not far off. I am persuaded the Lord will not be absent above 300 years longer.' "—RH, Feb. 14, 1854.

Comparing the cleansing with judgment, he asked, "What was that work of cleansing? Is the work of cleansing the Sanctuary fitly heralded by the first angel's message? In other words, Is it a work of judgment? For light on this subject, we shall be obliged to go to the type. Let us look at the type. See the high priest preparing himself to cleanse the Sanctuary; almost the first thing he did was to gird upon him the breast-plate of judgment. For what does he put that on? It certainly looks as though he was going to do a judgment work."—*Ibid.*

"Investigative Judgment" First Used

Though for many years Seventh-day Adventists have believed that James White first used the phrase "investigative judgment," recent study shows that Elon Everts employed it in a letter published in the *Review and Herald* and written on December 17, 1856. He suggested there was Bible evidence "that the righteous dead have been under investigative judgment since 1844." "I solemnly believe," he said, "that the judgment has been going on in the Heavenly Sanctuary since 1844, and that upon the righteous dead, from 'righteous Abel' down through patriarchs, prophets, martyrs, and all the saints who have fallen asleep in Jesus, judgment has been passing."—"Communication From Brother Everts," RH, Jan. 1, 1857.

Just four weeks later, James White used the term "investigative judgment" four times. The concept of the judging of the professed righteous was clear to him:

> For the time is come that judgment must begin at the house of God, and if it first begin at us, what shall the end be of them that obey not the gospel of God? And if the righteous scarcely be saved, where shall the ungodly and the sinner appear? 1 Peter 4:17, 18.
>
> This text we must regard as prophetic. That it applies to the last period of the church of Christ, seems evident from verses 5-7, 12, 13. In the judgment of the race of man, but two great classes are recognized—the righteous and the sinner, or ungodly. Each class has its time of judgment; and, according to the text, the judgment of the house, or church, of God comes first in order.
>
> Both classes will be judged before they are raised from the dead. The investigative judgment of the house, or church, of God will take place before the first resurrection; so will the judgment of the wicked

take place during the 1,000 years of Revelation 20, and they will be raised at the close of that period.—RH, Jan. 29, 1857.

White saw several reasons why the investigative judgment of the righteous would need to occur *before* the second coming of Christ:

> It is said of all the just, "Blessed and holy is he that hath part in the first resurrection," therefore all their cases are decided before Jesus comes to raise them from the dead. The judgment of the righteous is while Jesus offers His blood for the blotting out of sins. Immortal saints will reign with Christ 1,000 years in the judgment of the wicked. Rev. 20:4; 1 Cor. 6:2, 3. The saints will not only participate in the judgment of the world, but in judging fallen angels. See Jude 6.
>
> "Some men's sins [the righteous] are open beforehand, going before to judgment; and some men [the wicked] they follow after." 1 Tim. 5:24. That is, some men lay open, or confess their sins, and they go to judgment while Jesus' blood can blot them out, and the sins be remembered no more; while sins unconfessed, and unrepented of, will follow, and will stand against the sinner in that great day of judgment of 1,000 years.
>
> That the investigative judgment of the saints, dead and living, takes place prior to the second coming of Christ seems evident from the testimony of Peter. "Who shall give account to him that is ready to judge the quick [living] and the dead. For for this cause was the gospel preached also to them that are dead, that they might be judged according [in like manner] to men in the flesh, but live according to God in the spirit. But the end of all things is at hand: be ye therefore sober, and watch unto prayer." 1 Peter 4:5-7.
>
> It appears that the saints are judged while some are living, and others are dead. To place the investigative judgment of the saints after the resurrection of the just supposes the possibility of a mistake in the resurrection, hence the necessity of an investigation to see if all who were raised were really worthy of the first resurrection. But the fact that *all* who have part in that resurrection are "blessed and holy" shows that decision is passed on all the saints before the second coming of Christ.—*Ibid.*

The Blotting Out of Sins

Turning to Daniel's prophetic dream, White considered the blotting out of sins:

> The 2300 days [Daniel 8:14] reached to the cleansing of the Sanctuary, or to the great day of atonement in which the sins of all who shall have part in the first resurrection will be blotted out. These days terminated in 1844. We think the evidence clear that since that time the judgment of those who died subjects of the grace of God has been going on, while Jesus has been offering His blood for the blotting out of their sins.
>
> When are sins blotted out? Is it at the time when they are forgiven? We think not. We must look to the great day of atonement as the time

when Jesus offers His blood for the blotting out of sins. It is at the time of the cleansing of the Sanctuary. Said Peter to the wondering multitude who witnessed the lame man healed, "Repent ye therefore, and be converted, that your sins may be blotted out, when the times of refreshing shall come from the presence of the Lord; and he shall send Jesus Christ, which before was preached unto you: whom the heaven must receive until the times of restitution of all things, which God hath spoken by the mouth of all his holy prophets since the world began." Acts 3:19-21.

Here the time for blotting out of sins is placed forward just prior to the second appearing of Jesus. It is evidently the last great work in the ministry of Christ in the heavenly Sanctuary.—*Ibid.*

Judgment Before Resurrection

All Adventist pioneers agreed on the concept of a judgment of the righteous *before* their resurrection. The next year Uriah Smith wrote of "investigating the characters of mankind":

A moment's consideration of the events connected with the close of this dispensation will reveal to us the fact that the line of distinction between the righteous and the wicked must be drawn before our Saviour makes His appearance; and that consequently the work of investigating the characters of mankind, and determining to which class they respectively belong, whether to the righteous or the wicked, must take place ere probation closes.—RH, April 1, 1858.

Smith approached the subject of judgment in connection with the two great resurrections—of the righteous and of the wicked:

There are plainly brought to view in the Scriptures two resurrections, first, of the righteous, second, of the wicked. "The dead in Christ," says Paul, "shall rise first." 1 Thess. 4:16. Again, it was shown John that a certain class would be raised to reign with Christ, and that a thousand years thereafter the "rest of the dead" should come upon the breadth of the earth, compass the camp of the saints, and be destroyed by fire. Rev. 20. He tells us moreover that the living righteous at the coming of Christ will be changed to immortality in the twinkling of an eye, and caught up to meet the Lord. 1 Cor. 15:51-54.

In each of these cases, if previous to the time of their resurrection or change, there has been no investigation of the characters of the sleeping or living multitudes, how is it determined who are "the dead in Christ," who among the living crowds that throng the earth, are worthy of immortality, and who should be abandoned to the dreary, hopeless slumber of a thousand years?

One fact will here be apparent to every mind. It is that after the righteous dead are raised, the living saints changed and caught up to meet the Lord in the air, there exists no necessity for any further judgment in their case, *unless* it be admitted that there may possibly have been some mistake in the matter, and the holy garb of immortality been bestowed upon some unworthy object from whom it must be torn again, or that some unsanctified character has been called from his dusty bed, whose only portion should have been the second resurrection and the second death.

To suppose, we say, a judgment on the righteous after it has been decided who are righteous, and they have been raised, is to admit the possibility of a mistake in the matter. But from casting such an imputation on the divine government, we at least, must be excused.—*Ibid.*

J. N. Andrews also discussed a preresurrection judgment of the righteous, making use of Paul's clear statements in 1 Corinthians 15:

The trump of God sounds as the Saviour descends from Heaven. When that trump is heard, all the righteous are, in the twinkling of an eye, changed to immortality. There can be no examination after this to determine whether they shall be counted worthy of eternal life, for they have already laid hold upon it. From this it follows that the examination and decision of the cases of the righteous takes place before the advent of Christ. The resurrection of the righteous to immortality is decisive proof that they have already passed the test of the Judgment, and have been accepted of the Judge. That they are thus raised to immortality, the following texts plainly teach:

1 Cor. 15:42: "So also is the resurrection of the dead. It is sown in corruption; *it is raised in incorruption.*"

Verse 43: "It is sown in dishonor; *it is raised in glory;* it is sown in weakness; *it is raised in power.*"

Verse 44: "It is sown a natural body; *it is raised a spiritual body.* There is a natural body, and there is a spiritual body."

Verses 51, 52: "Behold, I shew you a mystery; We shall not all sleep, but we shall all be changed, in a moment, in the twinkling of an eye, at the last trump: for the trumpet shall sound, and the dead *shall be raised incorruptible,* and we shall be changed."

These passages are perfectly convincing. The resurrection of the saints is to immortal life, and they are made immortal in the very act of the resurrection. The decision of their cases is, therefore, passed before their resurrection, for the *nature* of their resurrection is declarative of their eternal salvation.—RH, Nov. 9, 1869.

Goodloe Harper Bell, pioneer educator among Seventh-day Adventists, commenting on the Sabbath school lessons in 1878, also supported the concept of an investigative judgment before Christ returns. He concluded that the cleansing of heaven's sanctuary was a cleansing of *the record of* sin.

"The heavenly sanctuary is polluted by the sins of God's people. They are borne by the High Priest of that sanctuary, and are also placed on record there. It is plain that when this sanctuary is cleansed, these sins will be removed. Christ will lay them off, and they will be blotted from the record; but this record cannot be blotted out until it has served its purpose. Out of the things written in this record the dead are to be judged. It is certain, then, that the cleansing of the sanctuary can never be accomplished until the books have been examined, and judgment has been passed upon all who have once entered the service of God; for not until then can their sins be blotted out.

"All who have ever entered the service of God have had their names entered in the book of life. The examination of the books of record will show what names are to be retained in the book of life, and what are to be blotted out. The names of all who have been unfaithful will be blotted out, while the names of those who, by their acts of repentance, confession, faith, and obedience, have made complete work of overcoming, will be retained. Rev. 3:5. Christ will confess their names before His Father and the holy angels, and present His blood as an atonement for their sins. Their sins will then be blotted out, and the heavenly record will be clean."—RH, Dec. 12, 1878.

Speaking to "believers in Christ," Uriah Smith said that "the Judgment really begins, and that portion of its work which most vitally concerns us is accomplished, before Christ appears."—RH, June 12, 1883. He made the following observation, still true today more than a hundred years later: "Strange to say, no system of belief appears which introduces this preliminary work of Judgment, and provides an appropriate time and place therefor, except that held by S.D. Adventists."—Ibid.

Smith referred to active opposition to the Adventist position and described Christ's work in heaven's sanctuary as "preliminary Judgment." "Why this opposition?" he asked. "We venture to suggest that the whole trouble is the connection of this view with the subject of the sanctuary; for in this alone we find the time and the place for the preliminary judgment which the very nature of the case shows to be so indispensable before Christ shall come."—Ibid.

Christ's work he termed as "cleansing," "atonement," and "the finishing of the mystery of God." "It is that portion of the ministry of our blessed Mediator which is performed in the second apartment, or most holy place, of the 'true tabernacle' on high. Heb. 8:1, 2. It is the cleansing of the sanctuary which was to commence at the end of the 2300 days. Dan. 8:14. It is the atonement, which concludes our Lord's work as priest, according to the type. Lev. 16:29-34. It is the finishing of the mystery of God, commencing with the sounding of the seventh angel (Rev. 10:7), a work introduced when that apartment of the temple in Heaven was opened which discloses to view the glorious ark of God's testament, containing the ten commandments. Rev. 11:19.

"By all these different modes of expression, and repeated Scripture affirmations, the same work is brought to view. It is a work of judgment; for it investigates character and decides cases. It is *the* work of judgment allotted to the last days just before the appearing of the Saviour. It is now going forward. The close of the 2300 days in 1844 brought us to its commencement. The period allotted to it will soon end, and its eternal decisions be all rendered. We cannot too earnestly urge upon the reader the importance of a constant and careful study of this grand theme, the antitypical sanctuary, and its cleansing."—*Ibid.*

Three Roles of Christ

The pioneers often spoke of three roles the Son of God fulfilled in three distinct periods of His act of salvation for mankind. J. N. Andrews said that "our Lord has three grand offices assigned Him in the Scriptures in the work of human redemption. When He was upon our earth at His first advent, He was that prophet of whom Moses spake, in Deuteronomy 18:15-19. See also Acts 3:22-26. When He ascended up to Heaven, He became a great High Priest, after the order of Melchisedec. Ps. 110; Heb. 8:1-6. But when He comes again, He is in possession of His kingly authority, as promised in the second Psalm. It is by virtue of this office of *king* that He judges mankind. Matt. 25:34, 40. The transition from our Lord's priesthood to His kingly office, precedes His second advent. Luke 19:11, 12, 15. It takes place when His Father sits in judgment, as described in Daniel 7:9-14."—RH, Dec. 7, 1869.

Uriah Smith also depicted Christ's threefold role:

> Three distinct and consecutive positions are assigned Him in the Scriptures, in connection with the work of human redemption.
> 1. His work upon this earth at His first advent was in fulfillment of the prediction by Moses fifteen hundred years before: "And the Lord said unto me, . . . I will raise them up a prophet from among their brethren like unto thee, and will put my words in his mouth; and he shall speak unto them all that I shall command him." Deut. 18:18, quoted and applied to Christ, in Acts 3:22, 23.
> 2. When, having suffered upon the cross as our sacrifice, and being raised from the dead for our justification, He ascended to the right hand of His Father, He became a great High Priest, after the order of Melchisedec. Ps. 110; Heb. 8:1-6.
> 3. But when He comes again, He is in possession of kingly authority, as promised in the second psalm, and bears upon His vesture the royal title "King of kings and Lord of lords." Rev. 19:16.

We thus find that His prophetic office was the subject of solemn promise (Deut. 18:15-18); His priesthood is established by an oath (Ps. 110:4); and His kingly office is the subject of a fixed decree, as declared in Psalm 2:6, 7.—RH, Feb. 10, 1885.

The Judgment Inseparable From the Gospel

Some have always wanted to separate judgment from the gospel. Such reasoning has led to extremes, however. Thus they have suggested either that God is too forgiving to punish, and we have no responsibility to obey, or we can be saved by observing rigid requirements. The pioneers regarded the judgment as inseparable from the gospel. Uriah Smith called attention to this fact as he commented on the first angel's message of Revelation 14:6, 7:

> This Judgment is a part of the gospel; for the everlasting gospel is what the angel was sent to preach, and all that the prophecy brings to view of his preaching is this appeal to all the people to fear God and give glory to Him; for the hour of His judgment is come.—RH, Jan. 6, 1874.

He continued with a historical perspective on the gospel:

> Among the great events of the gospel, the Judgment thus holds an important and prominent place. It transpires at the conclusion of human probation. It declares the result of the working of the plan of salvation for 6,000 years.
>
> The gospel is one gospel, but it embraces distinct and separate truths, which at different times become leading themes of its proclamation. Thus, in the first years of what is known as the gospel dispensation, the burden of evangelical preaching was a crucified and risen Saviour; or, the fact that Christ had appeared in the flesh as a sacrifice for men. In the days of the great Reformation, it was Justification through Christ, without the intervention of a human priesthood.
>
> As we draw near the end, when the Judgment is impending, and the everlasting kingdom of Christ is to be established, taking such only among the living as are ready to enter therein, this fact, as a matter of course, and from the very nature of the case, rises into prominence, and becomes the leading idea to be urged upon the attention of the people.—*Ibid.*

The Judgment and Today

Smith went on to emphasize why the judgment message has special significance for the present:

> The apostles did not proclaim the hour of God's judgment come. It would not have been true if they had proclaimed it. Instead of this, they pointed to the future for that event. Paul reasoned before Felix of a judgment, not come, but *to* come, sometime in the future. Acts

24:25. And he told the men of his generation, not that a day had come, but that one was appointed still in the future, for that purpose. Acts 17:31. He also expressly wrote to the believers in Thessalonica that Christians should not expect that day till after the long period of papal apostasy. 2 Thess. 2:3.—*Ibid.*

As for the Protestant Reformation, he said:

The reformers did not fulfill this prophecy. Martin Luther held and taught that the judgment would not come for 300 years from his day.—*Ibid.*

The First Angel of Revelation 14

Then Smith recalled the rise of the Advent movement in the nineteenth century, and the message that it preached:

But we come to our own time and find a movement which shook the churches of all Christendom. We find men moved as if by a divine impulse, giving utterance to a definite and specific proclamation through Europe, Asia and Africa; while a thousand ministers took up the theme in the more enlightened lands of England and America. We find them sending forth the tidings to every missionary station on the globe. . . .

Those who were engaged in preaching the soon coming of Christ between the years 1840 and 1844 claimed to be giving the first message of Revelation 14. And the movement answers to the prophecy in every particular.

1. It answers to it in time; for it has come forth at the very time when all prophecy and all signs show that the end is at hand.

2. It answers to it in the nature of the message proclaimed; for it points to the Judgment.

3. It answers to it in extent; for it has gone to all the world.

Now, no movement ever took place at the very time when such a movement was predicted to occur, and accomplished the very work specified in the prophecy, without being a fulfillment of that prophecy.

In the great Advent movement of the present generation, therefore, we have a fulfillment of the first message of Revelation 14, which announces the hour of God's judgment come.—*Ibid.*

Why a Judgment?

The judgment theme runs through the Bible. But unrepentant sinners naturally do not welcome such an event. The idea of punishment and justice would hardly comfort the wicked. But what about those who profess to be God's people: Why a judgment for them? Uriah Smith looked at this question:

But it may be asked, "Where is the need of any previous investigation? does not God know all men? does He not know His people? and can He not give them immortality at once through the exercise of His own omniscience?" We reverently admit that He could do this; but His Word informs us that He has not chosen to do so. If God by an act of His own omniscience decides all cases and visits rewards or punishments upon each "in a moment, in the twinkling of an eye," where is that process called "the judgment," which is so clearly revealed in the Bible? We appear before the judgment-seat of Christ to "receive [sentence for] the things done in the body" (2 Cor. 5:10); and it is expressly declared that when men are judged, they are judged (that is, decision is made and sentence is rendered) according to a record of their deeds kept in books which may be called the books of judgment. Rev. 20:12.

In the very opening scene of the judgment (Dan. 7:10) it is said, "And the books were opened"; and in the closing scene (Rev. 20:12) it also reads, "And the books were opened." Therefore what is experienced by the righteous and wicked at the coming of Christ does not proceed from the workings of God's omniscience at the moment exercised, but is the result of decisions previously arrived at in their cases.—RH, May 22, 1888.

In a statement made thirty years earlier, he had suggested reasons for the importance of the subject for our day:

Brethren, we are satisfied that this is the great subject for this time. The Judgment! The Judgment! Would that a voice might continually remind us that its solemn council is now in session, and its unalterable decisions passing upon our race. Reader, how does your case stand? Have you an interest in the Advocate who is pleading the cases of His children before His Father? Are you aware of a charge that yet stands against you unrepented of and unforgiven? Pass not over this subject lightly. Eternity is bound up in it. An endless and glorious life, or an eternal death, hang upon the issue. May the Lord help us to *feel* over it, and feeling to act—so act that our sins may be blotted from the book of His remembrance and our names, though unworthy, still stand in the golden characters of the book of life.—RH, April 8, 1858.

Present Truth

Viewing the theme of the judgment as the vital one for his generation, Smith compared and contrasted it with the message of the apostle Paul in his day:

The present truth in the days of the apostle Paul was that the Son of God, in the person of Jesus Christ, had just been to this earth, and by His death on the cross had made the great sacrifice which was able to redeem man, and purchase back his forfeited possession. Hence, the apostle declared that he determined to know nothing among those with whom he labored, "but Jesus Christ and him crucified." 1 Cor. 2:2. That is, he would labor to "make known" nothing else; this should be his constant theme, iterated and reiterated, till the glad tidings had gone to all men.

The present truth for this time is that this same Jesus, having now nearly accomplished the purpose for which He ascended to heaven, is about to return to this earth again to gather up the fruit of His long and merciful labors in behalf of the children of men; that His work as Mediator is almost finished; and that the primary division of the work of the judgment of the great day must take place before His priesthood ends; for the last work He performs as Mediator for His people is to confess their names before His Father and the holy angels (Rev. 3:5), and then their cases are forever decided.

A part of the work of Judgment must therefore precede the coming of Christ in the clouds of heaven; and if He is about thus to appear, the time has already come for this deciding Judgment work. And this is the startling feature of this truth—the time has come, and this Judgment work has been for even many years going forward. Ought not this truth then to be iterated and reiterated in the ears of the people, that the Judgment is now passing, and they all have a case, involving their interests for eternity pending there?—RH, March 23, 1886.

In Conclusion

The concept of judgment has been a part of 1884 from the beginning. After that year, however, the judgment concept was attached to heaven's sanctuary and Christ's work there. The pioneers emphasized several points.

1. Though Everts and White appear to have first used the term "investigative judgment" early in 1857, both Millerites and Seventh-day Adventist pioneers frequently spoke of judgment before Christ returns. William Miller joined his voice with the SDA pioneers shortly after the Disappointment in describing such a judgment in heaven.

2. They recognized the necessity of such a judgment to determine who would be resurrected at Christ's second coming, and who would await the second resurrection of the wicked to receive final punishment at the end of the one thousand years of Revelation 20.

3. The investigative judgment, they concluded, involved only those who had professed to accept the plan of salvation as fulfilled in the sacrifice of Christ for their sins.

4. The pioneers conceived of Christ in three roles in certain time frames: (1) as prophet (and finally Sacrifice, while on earth), (2) as high priest when He returned to heaven, and (3) as king when He comes to earth the second time.

5. They regarded the judgment as inseparable from the gospel as demonstrated in the first angels' message of Revelation 14:6, 7,

which called attention to the fact that "the hour of His judgment is come."

6. The judgment-hour message they held to have come at exactly the right time—not too soon or too late. It is an integral part of the proclamations of the three angels of Revelation 14.

* * * *

Ellen White testified to the investigative judgment in heaven's sanctuary in the following references:

The Great Controversy, pp. 479-491; *Patriarchs and Prophets,* pp. 357, 358; *The Story of Redemption,* p. 378.

* * * *

ARTICLES QUOTED IN THIS CHAPTER

James White
Jan. 29, 1857, The Judgment

J. N. Andrews
Nov. 9, 1869, The Order of Events in the Judgment (Series)
Dec. 7, 1869, The Order of Events in the Judgment
Feb. 8, 1870, The Order of Events in the Judgment

Uriah Smith
April 1, 1858, Synopsis of the Present Truth (Series)
April 8, 1858, Synopsis of the Present Truth
Jan. 6, 1874, The Hour of His Judgment Come
June 12, 1883, A Work of Judgment
Feb. 10, 1885, The Judgment of the Great Day
March 23, 1886, The Judgment Now Passing
May 22, 1888, The Investigative Judgment

David Arnold
December, 1849, The Shut Door Explained *(The Present Truth)*

J. N. Loughborough
Feb. 14, 1854, The Hour of His Judgment Come
Nov. 19, 1857, The Judgment

Joseph Bates
December, 1850, Midnight Cry in the Past

Goodloe Harper Bell
Dec. 12, 1878, Lessons for Bible Classes

8

Cleansing of the Sanctuary

Seventh-day Adventists have usually identified the cleansing of the sanctuary mentioned in Daniel 8:14 with the investigative judgment in heaven's sanctuary. Because cleansing and judgment are parallel, but perhaps not identical in all details, we now consider how the pioneers viewed the cleansing.

What Is the "Cleansing"?

James White explained in 1854 what it is. "The *event* to transpire at the end of the 2300 days is the cleansing of the Sanctuary. That the tabernacle of God is the Sanctuary of the Bible, a multitude of texts directly testify. Ex. 36:1-6; Lev. 4:6; 16:33; Num. 4:15; Ps. 78:54, 69; Heb. 8:1, 2. That the cleansing of the Sanctuary is the work of a high priest, performed by blood, and not with fire, is also a matter of certainty. Lev. 16; Heb. 9.

"The work of cleansing the Sanctuary is not that of a king taking vengeance on his adversaries, but that of a priest concluding his work in the tabernacle of God. Hence, this work must precede the Second Advent, and be accomplished ere the priestly work of our Lord is closed in the Sanctuary of God. Until that point of time, the wrath of God is stayed by the intercession of our great High Priest. When that point is reached, the sins of the host or church, having been transferred from the Sanctuary to the anti-typical scapegoat, and the saints of God being all sealed, the wrath of God without mixture of mercy is poured out, and the adversaries of the Lord are destroyed with an utter destruction."—RH, Dec. 5, 1854.

When Is the "Cleansing"?

Some years later J. N. Andrews told when he considered it would occur. "The cleansing of the sanctuary predicted in Daniel is to take place in the closing part of the gospel dispensation. But the sanctuary of this dispensation is in Heaven. Moreover, the sanctuary of the new covenant is to be cleansed for the same reason that the sanctuary of the first covenant was cleansed. This cleansing takes place of necessity as our High Priest closes up His work, so that the heavenly sanctuary is cleansed at the very time that this takes place with the sanctuary of Daniel."—RH, Dec. 30, 1873.

Cleansing and Judgment

Continuing his review of the work of Christ in heaven, note how Andrews related "cleansing" and "investigative judgment." "It is announced by the proclamation of Revelation 14:6, 7, that the hour of God's judgment is come. It is marked by the ending of the prophetic periods. This judgment scene takes place within the second apartment by the ark of God. Rev. 11:18, 19. The scene is described in Daniel 7:9-14, where the Ancient of Days sits in judgment, and the Son of man approaches His throne and closes His priestly work by being crowned King of kings. Here is the place for the blotting out of sins as each case is examined before God; and this blotting out of sins is the grand idea of cleansing the sanctuary of God.

"Now Christ does not approach the Father in the manner described in Daniel 7:13, 14, at His ascension, for the Father did not then sit in judgment; nor does He thus approach Him in coming to our earth at the second advent, for the Father is not here on earth when the Son descends; and, moreover, the Son comes to our earth as King (Matt. 25:31; Luke 19:12, 15), and it is at this tribunal that He receives His kingdom and glory. There is but one consistent view that can be taken of this judgment scene in Daniel 7 at which Christ is crowned, and that is that it is the work of investigative judgment in the second apartment of the heavenly sanctuary."—*Ibid.*

In an article the next year, he actually considered the sanctuary cleansing as identical with the work of the investigative judgment. "The work of the judgment is divided into two parts. The first part is the *investigative* judgment, which takes place in the heavenly sanctuary, God the Father sitting in judgment. The second part is the *execution* of the judgment, and is committed wholly to Christ, who comes to our earth to accomplish this work. John 5:22-27; Jude 14, 15. It is while the investigative judgment is in session that the cleansing of the sanctuary takes place. Or, to speak more accurately, the cleansing of the sanctuary is identical with the work of the investigative judgment."—RH, March 10, 1874.

Andrews used Scripture copiously to support an investigative judgment and the cleansing of the sins of the righteous from heaven's record prior to Christ's second advent:

> This part of the judgment is described in Daniel 7:9-14. God the Father sits upon the throne of judgment. Those who stand before the Father are the angels. Compare Rev. 5:11. It is not upon earth, for the Father does not come to our earth. It is before the second advent of Christ, for Christ comes to our earth as a king sitting upon His own throne (Matt. 25:31, 34; Luke 19:12, 15; 2 Tim. 4:1), but this tribunal of the Father is the very place where He is crowned king. Dan. 7:13, 14. It is the time and place where our Lord concludes His priestly office, and must, therefore, be in the second apartment of the sanctuary above. Rev. 10:7; 11:15; 18, 19.
>
> When the Saviour comes, He gives immortality to the righteous dead. 1 Cor. 15:23, 51-55; 1 Thess. 4:15-17. The rest of the dead are left until the resurrection of the unjust. Rev. 20. But those who are thus made immortal were *previously accounted worthy* of that great salvation. Luke 20:35. There can be no examination afterward to ascertain whether they shall be saved or lost, for they are put in possession of eternal life at the moment when the trumpet sounds. And such, also, is the case with the living righteous. They are changed to immortality in the same moment with the dead in Christ. 1 Thess. 4:15-17. These are previously judged worthy of this great salvation (Luke 21:36), and can never afterward be subjected to trial for the determination of this point. The decision who shall have eternal life has, therefore, been made before Christ descends to execute the judgment.
>
> The books are examined before the deliverance of the saints. Dan. 12:1. The opening of the books is described in Daniel 7:9, 10. The book of life shows who have ever set out in the service of God. Luke 10:20; Phil. 4:3. The book of God's remembrance shows the record of their faithfulness in His cause, and whether they have made clean work in overcoming. Mal. 3:16. Other books contain the record of men's evil deeds. Rev. 20:12, 13.
>
> As the object of this final work in the sanctuary is to determine who are worthy of everlasting life, no cases will come before this tribunal except those who have had their names entered in the book of life. All others are left out of this investigation as having never become partakers in Christ's atoning work. The investigation will determine who have overcome their sins; and these will have their sins blotted from the record, and their names retained in the book of life. It will also determine who have not overcome and these will have their names blotted from the book of life, Revelation 3:5, and their sins will be retained in the record, to be visited with retribution in the resurrection to damnation.—*Ibid.*

The Living Righteous and Cleansing

Placing the cleansing of heaven's sanctuary in a present context, he expressed why he saw it so important for *living* believers in Jesus Christ to understand His ministry in heaven right now.

> The proclamation of the third angel, which is made while Christ is closing up His work in the sanctuary, is designed to prepare the living for the decision of the Judgment. When the cases of the living are reached, probation closes up forever. The decree goes forth from the throne of God, "He that is unjust, let him be unjust still; . . . and he that is holy, let him be holy still." Rev. 22:11. The sins of the overcomers being blotted out, and the sanctuary cleansed, the Son of God is no longer needed as a great High Priest. He therefore ceases from that office forever and becomes a king for the deliverance and glorification of His people, and for the destruction of all transgressors. Dan. 7:13, 14. Satan, the author of sin, receives its dreadful burden when the work in the sanctuary is closed and will bear it with him to the lake of fire.
>
> It is of infinite consequence to us who live in the time when Christ is closing up His priesthood, that we understand the work which He is performing, and that we so walk in the light as to share in His great salvation.—*Ibid.*

At about the same time Uriah Smith also used the word "judgment" to refer to the cleansing in heaven's sanctuary:

> When the Scriptures speak of accomplished events, they so express it, as of the two witnesses, Rev. 11:7: "When they shall have finished their testimony," or of Christ, 1 Cor. 15:24, "when he shall have delivered up the Kingdom." But when they say, "Then shall be great tribulation," Matt. 24:21, it means that it shall then begin and continue and when they say, "Then shall that wicked be revealed," 2 Thess. 2:8, it means then shall begin the period during which He will stand revealed before the world. So, "then shall the sanctuary be cleansed" simply refers to the time when the work shall commence.
>
> Therefore are we held inevitably to the conclusion that at the end of the 2300 days, in the autumn of 1844, the ministration of the sanctuary above was changed from the holy to the most holy place. Then the temple of God was opened in Heaven, and there was seen in His temple the ark of His testament. Rev. 11:19. There the Ancient of days then placed His throne and "did sit," as the prophet Daniel saw. Dan. 7:9. Then, escorted by the retinue of holy angels, Christ, our Priest and Mediator, moved into the inner temple to receive from His Father the result of His long work of mediation for man. Dan. 7:13, 14. Then opened the solemn Judgment scene of verses 9 and 10 of Daniel 7.* Then the seventh angel sounded, and the work of finishing the mystery of God began. Rev. 10:7. These are the sublime events involved in the cleansing of the sanctuary which then commenced.—RH, Aug. 10, 1876.

---

*We observe that the pioneers taught the judgment based on Daniel 7, perhaps even more than on Daniel 8:14, which gives the time and the dimension of cleansing the sanctuary.

The Adventist Position Is Unique

Seventh-day Adventists are alone among Christian bodies today in teaching an investigative judgment. Smith spoke of its uniqueness and of how others had tried to discount it:

> We know of no system of belief which has a place for this preliminary work of judgment, except that held by S.D. Adventists. It has been a source of perplexity to many, and to meet it, they have been obliged to resort to such unscriptural conclusions as these:
>
> 1. That all the race, good and bad, are raised indiscriminately together; whereas the Bible plainly declares that there are a thousand years between the resurrection of the righteous and that of the wicked. Rev. 20:5.
>
> 2. That when the righteous are raised, they are raised mortal, judged and then changed; whereas the Bible assigns no place for any such work of investigative judgment after Christ appears, and moreover, explicitly declares that the righteous are raised in power, in glory, with spiritual bodies, and in incorruption. 1 Cor. 15:42-44.— RH, Aug. 17, 1876.

Cleansing Is a Judgment

Also Smith agreed with Andrews regarding the parallel of the cleansing of the sanctuary with judgment:

> The cleansing of the sanctuary is a work of judgment. A few considerations will make this proposition plain. The priesthood of Christ continues up to the time when He takes His own throne as king. He passes directly from the first position to the second; and when He takes His position as king, His work as priest is done. Now, His work as priest, being for the purpose of gathering out from the human family a people for His name and kingdom, His priestly office cannot close till this result is declared.
>
> When He ends His work, it will be decided who have availed themselves of His mediation, and have thus become His people. It is the putting away of sin that determines this; but this is the very work that Christ performs in the most holy in the conclusion of His ministry. He here puts away the sins of His people; and this is the cleansing of the sanctuary.—*Ibid.*

The pioneers taught that human beings do not appear in person at the judgment, but will be there through the records in heaven. Smith continued:

> This involves an examination of the books; for the rule that God has laid down in this matter is that all judgment shall be rendered according to each man's works as they stand upon the record. "And the dead," says John, "were judged out of those things which were written in the books, according to their works." Rev. 20:12. From the reference in this and numerous other passages, to the books, the book of life, the names or the things written therein, and the blotting out to

take place, but one conclusion can be drawn; and that is that a faithful record is kept of each one's actions, the thoughts, words and deeds that make up the texture of his character, and the course of his life.—*Ibid.*

The idea of cleansing and judgment he employed somewhat interchangeably:

> The cleansing of the sanctuary involves the examination of the records of all the deeds of our lives. It is an investigative Judgment. Every individual of every generation from the beginning of the world thus passes in review before the great tribunal above. So Daniel, describing the opening of this scene, calls it a work of Judgment, and expressly notices the fact that the books were opened. Dan. 7:9, 10.
>
> This work has been going forward in the sanctuary above since the end of the prophetic period in 1844. Beginning, according to the natural order, with the earliest generation, the work of examination passes on down through all the records of time, and closes with the living. Then the sealing message, Revelation 7, will have performed its work, and all antecedent questions being determined, all cases decided, everything will be ready for the coming of the Lord.—*Ibid.*

Sacrifice and Atonement

Uriah Smith became involved in an exchange of views with a Seventh-day Baptist* minister, J. W. Morton, on the distinction between Christ's sacrifice and the application of that sacrifice. Referring to Hebrews 10:10, Smith said, "What Christ did 'once for all' was to give Himself upon the cross, a sacrifice of such infinite merit as to be able to cancel the guilt of the whole world. Through this sacrifice every sinner must come to God."—RH, April 17, 1888. He then quoted J. N. Andrews. "On this point we have ever felt to adopt the language of the late Elder Andrews. Speaking of the fact that Christ obtains from God the pardon of the sinner through His blood, He said, 'Whether by its actual presentation or by virtue of its merits, we need not stop to inquire.' "—*Ibid.*

Thus, Smith continued, "Christ shed His blood, and the merits of that sacrifice He pleads before the Father for the sinner. How often does He do this?—As often as a sinner comes to Him."—*Ibid.* Objecting to Morton's contention that Christ has pleaded His blood only once before the Father, he argued, "The trouble with him, as with religious teachers generally, is that he confounds the sacrifice with the ministration, the offering of the victim with the atonement. Though Christ died once for all upon the cross, the virtue of that

---

* In the earliest days, Seventh Day Baptists spelled their name this way, but later dropped the hyphen and capitalized Day.

sacrifice is often called into requisition. It is applied in the case of every penitent sinner who comes to God through Jesus Christ."— *Ibid.*

Writing again in 1894, Smith referred to a distinction the pioneers often made between Christ's sacrificial death and the application of its benefits. Though the cross provided completely for man's sins, he had to accept that provision. The atonement, they said, is not complete until the investigative judgment has determined that fact. Such a conclusion avoids two extreme positions—one, that Christ's death will automatically save *all*, and two, that His death was only for those predestined to be saved. Both extremes would leave out the right of the sinner to choose, as well as any necessity for living an obedient life. It would make a farce of the ten commandments of God, and would release us from any requirements to do what is right. Smith said:

"On the cross Christ offered Himself as the *sacrifice*," "In heaven He pleads His blood as *priest*, and makes the atonement. Therefore, though He bore on the cross the sins of the world, that is, made a sacrifice which would be of sufficient merit to cover and cancel all the sins of every person who has ever lived, or is to live, on this earth, it does not follow that all will be saved; for all will not come to Him that they might have life. John 5:40. But for all who will come to Him and seek and accept His pardon, He will grant it on the strength of His sacrifice, and make atonement for their sins when the time comes for His mediation for the world to close and probation to end." *—RH, Jan. 30, 1894.

Judicial and Executive Judgment

Roswell F. Cottrell, in 1884 distinguished between judicial and executive judgment. That is, the judging and the carrying out of the sentence. Concluding that the Lord had overruled the Disappointment and its aftermath for good, he felt that the whole experience had allowed Adventists time to learn the truth.

> At the close of the 2300 days in 1844, a message was sounding forth throughout the earth, "Fear God, and give glory to him, for the hour of his judgment is come." It was a message of the word of God promised in prophecy. Rev. 14:6, 7. It was announced as promised. The promise being once redeemed, it does not remain still due. That work will not be repeated. It was God's work, and needs no mending.
>
> But the inference that the Lord must come to earth at the end of the days was human. It was founded in ignorance; yet it did not

---

* Note that Smith uses the word *atonement* in the sense of *applying* the blood shed on Calvary.

hinder the work of the Lord, but was overruled to help it forward. That was not the last work of the gospel, as it was then supposed to be; and the cleansing of the sanctuary was not the cleansing of the earth by fire, as it was believed. In the fulfillment of the prophetic program, time has been given in which to learn the truth concerning the sanctuary and its cleansing, the opening of the judgment in heaven (Dan. 7:9), and the last message of the gospel on earth. Rev. 14:9-12.—*RH*, April 22, 1884.

Then he looked at what he called the "two principal parts in the Judgment":

There are two principal parts in the Judgment in respect to both classes, the righteous and the wicked; namely, the judicial, or investigative, and the executive. In the former, decisions are made; in the latter, the decisions are executed. The execution of the Judgment in respect to the saved takes place in a moment, in the twinkling of an eye, at the coming of Christ and the first resurrection. Luke 14:14; 1 Cor. 15:23, 51, 52; 1 Thess. 4:16, 17; Rev. 20:4-6. This being the case, the books must be opened, and the decision for life or for death in each case made before the coming of Christ.

In harmony with this, the opening scene of the Judgment is described in Daniel 7:9. This scene transpires in heaven before the Ancient of Days. "God is judge himself." Ps. 50:6. The Son of man is brought near before Him; and when His intercessions for His people as priest are ended, and their sins blotted out, He receives the kingdom and returns to earth as King. Rev. 14:14, 19:11.—*Ibid.*

Cottrell concluded by saying:

The closing of the priesthood of Christ, the cleansing of the sanctuary, takes place within the second vail; and as soon as the sins of His people are all blotted out, He receives His kingdom and returns to the earth to execute judgment, and give eternal life to all whose sins have been blotted out.

The cleansing of the sanctuary is the final removal of the sins of all the saved. But when it is decided that their sins are forever canceled, it is decided that they are accounted worthy to obtain the world to come and the resurrection to eternal life. Hence when the time appointed for the cleansing of the sanctuary arrived, the message declaring that "the hour of his judgment is come" was true.—*Ibid.*

The Bible and "Investigative Judgment"

The pioneers regarded the cleansing of the sanctuary as a work or process of judgment. Frequently they interchanged the terms and sometimes considered them as synonymous. However, they recognized that the term "investigative judgment" does not appear in Scripture.

Uriah Smith explained:

We do not claim that we find this term in the Bible, but we adopt it as being the most clearly expressive of the nature of this portion of the Judgment work; and a moment's thought must convince anyone that just such a Judgment, or investigation of character, and decision of cases for salvation or destruction, *must* precede the coming of Christ, inasmuch as when Christ appears there is no time allotted for investigation of character, but in a moment, in the twinkling of an eye, the two classes, righteous and wicked, both dead and living, are divided, the righteous being made immortal, and the wicked given over to destruction.—RH, Aug. 2, 1887.

The Meaning of *Tsadaq*

He provided a further thought on the word translated "cleansed" in Daniel 8:14:

The word rendered "cleansed" (margin, "justified"), in Daniel 8:14, is *tsadaq;* and one of the definitions given to this word in Bagster's Hebrew lexicon is, "to be purified"; and Daniel 8:14 is referred to as the passage where it has this meaning. Bagster refers also to the Septuagint and Vulgate as using the word in the same sense. This is the term which Paul uses in Hebrews 9:23, when speaking of the cleansing of both the worldly and the heavenly Sanctuary. He says: "It was therefore necessary that the patterns of things in the heavens should be purified with these; but the heavenly things themselves with better sacrifices than these." The Greek word here used is *katharizo,* which is defined, *"to cleanse, to render pure; by metonymy, to cleanse* from sin, *purify by an expiatory offering, make expiation for,* Heb. 9:22, 23."

Thus we see that there is complete harmony between the Hebrew and the Greek, and between the Old and New Testaments on this subject. Daniel uses a word which means "to purify."

"Unto two thousand and three hundred days, then shall the sanctuary be purified." And Paul follows with a comment saying that "the heavenly things themselves" (by which term he refers to the heavenly Sanctuary, Heb. 8:2; 9:23) must be "purified." And this purification is a "cleansing from sin by an expiatory offering."

The words used in the original convey the idea more accurately than the English translation; for the English word "to cleanse" suggests first the idea of removing literal or physical impurity, and so gives an objector a chance to quibble over the idea that there is anything physically impure in heaven; but the words used in the Hebrew and Greek do not admit the idea of cleansing from physical uncleanness, but only from the defilement of sin; and this is not accomplished by soap and sand, but by the blood of an offering. Of sins only is the Sanctuary to be cleansed.—RH, March 13, 1888.

In Conclusion

The pioneers generally taught that the cleansing of the sanctuary and the investigative judgment are synonymous. They

CLEANSING OF THE SANCTUARY

agreed that the cleansing is to take place at the closing of the gospel dispensation, and that it involved the only sanctuary in existence at that time—the heavenly one.

Also they accepted that God will finally blot out sins from the heavenly records before the Second Coming. The earthly sanctuary of the Old Testament had its accumulated sins removed once a year on the Day of Atonement. But in the one in heaven, it will happen only once at the end of time.

The Seventh-day Adventist Church has a unique position on this teaching in the religious world. The early denominational leaders concluded that the death of Christ made *provision* for confessed sin, and His work as our high priest in judgment makes *application* of the benefits of His sacrifice. They understood this as in harmony with the Old Testament sanctuary services. Also they regarded the cleansing as purifying both the sanctuary and the sinner from sin.

* * * *

Ellen White spoke of the cleansing of the sanctuary in the following references:

The Great Controversy, pp. 421-436, 479, 480; *Selected Messages*, book 1, pp. 343, 344; *Early Writings*, pp. 42, 43, 243, 250, 251, 253, 254-257; *Life Sketches*, p. 278; *The Story of Redemption*, pp. 378, 379.

* * * *

ARTICLES QUOTED IN THIS CHAPTER

James White
    Dec. 5, 1854, The Sanctuary

J. N. Andrews
    Dec. 30, 1873, The Sanctuary of the Bible
    March 10, 1874, The Sanctuary of the Bible

Uriah Smith
    Aug. 10, 1876, The Sanctuary (Series)
    Aug. 17, 1876, The Sanctuary
    Aug. 2, 1887, J. W. Morton and the Sanctuary Question
    March 13, 1888, Then Shall the Sanctuary Be Cleansed
    April 17, 1888, Not the Very Image
    Jan. 30, 1894, The Atonement

R. F. Cottrell
    April 22, 1884, The Cleansing of the Sanctuary

9

The Two Goats

In the previous chapter we considered the cleansing of the sanctuary, which was accomplished, in symbol, by the application of the blood of the Lord's goat in the holy place on the Day of Atonement, and at the altar of burnt offering in the court. Remember that the priest brought two goats without blemish and cast lots upon them to determine the use to be made of each of them. One became the sacrifice for sin; the other was called the scapegoat, and served a far different purpose. The comments of the pioneers on the scapegoat are pertinent to our study.

Christ Not the Scapegoat

Uriah Smith carefully listed several reasons why he believed the scapegoat could *not* symbolize Christ:

> 1. If Christ, in bearing the sin of the world, fulfilled the antitype of the scapegoat, He must have accomplished it at the crucifixion; for Peter says of Him, "Who his own self bare our sins in his own body on the tree." 1 Peter 2:24. But in the type the goat was not sent away till *after* the cleansing of the Sanctuary; hence the antitype of this work cannot be performed till after the termination of the 2300 days; for it is not till after those days have ended that the Sanctuary is cleansed. Dan. 8:14; Heb. 9:23. It is therefore impossible to carry this work back to the crucifixion of Christ, which was even before He commenced His ministration in the Sanctuary above; and therefore He cannot be the antitype of the scapegoat.
>
> 2. Christ is our great High Priest, the minister of the Sanctuary; but the goat is something to be sent away *by* the priest: therefore he cannot be the priest himself: in other words, he cannot in this dispensation be Christ; but he must be a being whom Christ, after He has loaded him with the sins borne from the Sanctuary, can *send away*

into a land not inhabited.

3. The goat was sent away *from* Israel into a land not inhabited, to be heard of no more forever. But Christ will dwell in the midst of His people, the true Israel of faith.

4. It is impossible that two goats, one of which was chosen by the Lord, and is called the Lord's, and was for a sin offering, while the other is not so called, but was left to perform an entirely different office—it is impossible that these both should typify the same person.—RH, March 18, 1858.

The Devil the Scapegoat

After ruling out Christ as the scapegoat, he asked the obvious question: "Who then can it be?" "The Devil," he answered, and followed with several reasons for such a conclusion:

1. We know of only two beings which anyone has ever thought could possibly be typified by the scapegoat; and these are Christ and Satan. We have shown above that the goat cannot be a type of Christ; we must therefore look to the Devil for its fulfillment.

2. The Hebrew word for scapegoat, as given in the margin of Leviticus 16:8, is *Azazel.** On this verse, Jenks in his Comprehensive Commentary remarks, "Scapegoat. . . . Spencer after the oldest opinion of the Hebrews and Christians thinks *Azazel* is the *name of the Devil.* . . . The Syriac has, *Azazel,* the angel (strong one) who revolted." The Devil is here evidently pointed out. Thus we have the definition of the Scripture term in two ancient languages, with the oldest opinion of the Christians in favor of the view that the scapegoat is a type of Satan.

3. In the common acceptation of the word, the term, scapegoat, is applied to any miserable vagabond who has become obnoxious to the claims of justice; and while it is revolting to all our conceptions of the character and glory of Christ, to apply this term to Him, it must strike everyone as a very appropriate designation of the Devil, who is styled in Scripture, the accuser, adversary, angel of the bottomless pit, Beelzebub, Belial, dragon, enemy, evil spirit, father of lies, murderer, prince of devils, serpent, tempter, etc., etc.

4. Our fourth reason for this position is the very striking manner in which it harmonizes with the events to transpire in connection with the cleansing of the heavenly Sanctuary, as far as revealed to us in the Scriptures of truth.—*Ibid.*

Smith then compared the Old Testament use of the two goats with Christ's sacrificial death, and His ministry in heaven's sanctuary:

We behold in the type, 1. The sin of the transgressor imparted to

---

*Crosier, in the *Day-Star Extra,* February 7, 1846, laid the Biblical basis for the Seventh-day Adventist belief that the scapegoat is the devil.

the victim. 2. We see that sin borne in by the priest in the blood of the offering into the Sanctuary. 3. On the tenth day of the seventh month we see the priest with the blood of the sin offering for the people remove all these sins from the Sanctuary, and lay them upon the head of the scapegoat. 4. The goat bears them way into a land not inhabited.

Answering to these events in the type, we behold in the antitype, 1. The great offering for the world made on Calvary. 2. The sins of all those who avail themselves of the merits of Christ's shed blood, by faith in Him, in that blood are borne into the Sanctuary. 3. After Christ, the minister of the true tabernacle [Hebrews 8:2], has finished His ministration, He will remove the sins of His people from the Sanctuary, and lay them upon the head of their author, the antitypical scapegoat, the Devil. 4. The Devil will be sent away with them into a land not inhabited.

If we want a description of this event in plain terms, we find it in Revelation 20:1-3: "And I saw an angel come down from heaven having the key of the bottomless pit, and a great chain in his hand. And he laid hold on the dragon, that old serpent, which is the Devil and Satan, and bound him a thousand years, and cast him into the bottomless pit, and shut him up, and set a seal upon him, that he should deceive the nations no more till the thousand years should be fulfilled."—*Ibid.*

The sending of the scapegoat into the wilderness Smith regarded as a graphic representation of Satan being cast into the bottomless pit, awaiting his final destruction:

Now we would ask, What could be more fitting than that the author and instigator of all sin should receive the guilt of those transgressions which he has incited mortals to commit, but of which they have repented, back upon his own head? And what could be a more striking antitype of the ancient ceremony of sending away the scapegoat into the wilderness, than the act of the mighty angel in binding Satan and casting him into the bottomless pit at the commencement of the thousand years.

This is a point of transcendent interest to every believer. Then the sins of God's people will be borne away to be remembered no more forever. Then he who instigated them will have received them back again. Then the serpent's head will have been bruised by the seed of the woman.—*Ibid.*

Predestination and Universalism

Dealing with two extreme positions, namely (1) that Christ died only for those predestined to be saved and (2) that He died for everyone, whether they accept His sacrifice or not, Smith asked:

For whom did Christ die? For a chosen few only, or for all? Evidently for all, otherwise all could not have an opportunity of repentance. "Well then," says one who is wedded to the pleasures of sin, "if sin can be suffered for but once, and Christ has suffered for my sins, what have I to fear? There is no suffering for sin for me to endure. I will therefore cull all the enjoyment I can from the pleasures of this world, and on the threshold of eternity I will take my stand beside the holiest saint that ever lived, and claim an equal right with him to the glories of heaven; for Christ suffered for me as well as for him; and therefore I am as free."

This is exactly the issue of the view taken; but the staunchest Universalism would require nothing better. Unless therefore we wish to yield the specific teachings of the Bible and become Universalists at once, we must abandon this theory. But its advocates may still contend that the wicked are exceptions, but that certainly sins that have been *pardoned* can never after be occasion of suffering to any being. But if when sins are pardoned that is the last of them, we would inquire how it happens that those very sins are transferred to the Sanctuary, and impurity imputed to it on their account. That this is so is one of the plainest teachings of the Bible.—*Ibid.*

Cleansing Only by Blood

A few years later James White reviewed two important points:

1. The earthly sanctuary was cleansed by blood.
2. The heavenly sanctuary must be cleansed by better sacrifices, that is, by the blood of Christ. It is plain, then, that the idea of cleansing the sanctuary by fire has no support in the Bible.*—RH, March 22, 1870.

Of the sanctuary he stated:

It was unclean in this sense only: the sins of men had been borne into it through the blood of sin offering, and they must be removed. This fact can be grasped by every mind.—*Ibid.*

Why a Scapegoat?

Then White turned his attention to the function of the scapegoat, offering specific arguments why it could not represent Christ:

The next event of that day, after the sanctuary was cleansed, was the putting of all the iniquities and transgressions of the children of Israel upon the scapegoat, and sending him away into a land not inhabited, or of separation. It is supposed by almost everyone that this goat typified Christ in some of His offices, and that the type was fulfilled at the first advent. From this opinion I must differ, because,

1. That the goat was not sent away till after the high priest *had made an end* of cleansing the sanctuary. Lev. 16:20, 21. Hence that event cannot meet its antitype till after the end of the 2300 days.

---

*That blood, and not fire, cleansed the sanctuary Crosier strongly argued in 1846. It supported his argument that the sanctuary was not the earth, and that the cleansing had to do with sin.

2. It was sent away from Israel into the wilderness, a land not inhabited; to receive them. If our blessed Saviour is its antitype, He also must be sent away from His people to a land not inhabited, but not to the grave; for the goat was sent away alive; nor into heaven, for that is not an uninhabited land.

3. The goat received and retained all the iniquities of Israel; but when Christ appears the second time, he will be "without sin."

4. The goat received the iniquities from the hands of the priest, and he *sent it away*. As Christ is the priest, the goat must be something else besides Himself which He can *send away*.

5. This was one of two goats, chosen for that day, of which one was the Lord's, and was offered for a sin offering; but the other was not called the Lord's, neither offered as a sacrifice. Its only office was to receive the iniquities from the priest, after he had cleansed the sanctuary from them, and bear them into a land not inhabited, leaving the sanctuary, priest, and people behind, and free from their iniquities. Lev. 16:7-10, 22.

6. The Hebrew name of the scapegoat, as will be seen from the margin of verse 8, is *Azazel*. . . .

7. At the appearing of Christ, as taught in Revelation 20, Satan is to be bound and cast into the bottomless pit, which act and place are significantly symbolized by the ancient high priest's sending the scapegoat into a separate and uninhabited wilderness.

8. Thus we have the Scripture, the definition of the name in two ancient languages, both spoken at the same time, and the oldest opinion of the Christians in favor of regarding the scapegoat as the type of *Satan.—Ibid.*

The Scapegoat as Satan

J. H. Waggoner added his voice to the belief that the scapegoat represents Satan: "In Revelation 20, there is something that bears a striking analogy to the action of the High Priest in regard to the scapegoat, and is, doubtless, a fulfillment of that type."—RH, July 7, 1874. He believed that "by reference to the Scripture use of the term *abyss* (rendered bottomless pit), we find the very idea of Leviticus 16:21, 22, carried out, for it is literally a desert waste, void, or land not inhabited."—*Ibid.*

Waggoner saw a "perfect fulfillment" of the Old Testament types or symbols. "Two facts only need notice to show the perfect fulfillment of the types in the scripture under consideration. (1) Satan is called the prince of the power of the air. By his creation as an exalted angel he has the power of traversing the air as well as the earth. To deprive him of that power and confine him to the earth would fulfill Revelation 20. (2) When Satan is bound, at the coming of Christ, the earth will be desolated, and left without an inhabitant."—*Ibid.*

Therefore he concluded that "after the atonement is made with the blood of the sin offering, the sin itself still exists, and falls somewhere else. In the type it was laid on the scapegoat; in the antitype, on the devil. And when he is destroyed, sin perishes with him; it is, in his extinction, literally 'done away,' or obliterated.' It has no more a record in the Word of God, nor a place in the universe. In this sense only has the scapegoat, or Satan, anything to do with the atonement. It is the blood that makes atonement. See Lev. 17:11; Heb. 9:22."—*Ibid.*

Why a Perfect Goat to Represent Satan?

Uriah Smith had more to say about the scapegoat in response to a correspondent to the *Review* who inquired why Scripture should employ a perfect goat to symbolize Satan. His answer:

1. Satan was not always the reprobate that he now is. Once he was one of the anointed cherubim, next in position, dignity, and perfection to the Son of God Himself. This we gather from the declarations of Isaiah and Ezekiel.

2. When the goats were selected on the day of atonement, one to be a sacrifice to the Lord, the other to be the scapegoat, it was not decided which goat was to perform either office till the lots were cast upon them. They must therefore both be without defect or blemish, that the lot for the Lord might appropriately fall on either one. . . .

3. The scapegoat having once been selected, it never after performed any office involving dignity or honor, or calling for any thing which would symbolize perfection of life or character. It was loaded with sins and thus made abominable in God's sight, and with its load of guilt and execration was hurried out of the camp into the wilderness, where it miserably perished afar from the children of Israel and the habitations of man. So will Satan at last receive the load of all that amount of sin which he has incited men to commit, from which they have freed themselves by penitence and confession, thus leaving them with the originator and instigator of sin, and with them he will miserably perish outside the camp of the saints.

4. This can never be true of Christ. That is, Christ never is to perish with the sins of His people upon Him. It fell to His lot to bear sins once. But this was when He was nailed to the tree, and bore the sins of the world as a *sacrifice*, preliminary to His work as Mediator in the sanctuary above. . . .

5. This consideration also answers another objection which is proposed by some, namely, that Satan can have no part to act in the work of the atonement. This objection is, as we view it, based on a misapprehension; for Satan does not have any part to act in making the atonement. The atonement is all made, sins are remitted, the records of the evil deeds of God's people are blotted out, and they are forever freed from them, and these sins are all borne from the sanctuary, before ever Satan is called into requisition at all. God then simply uses him as the vehicle by which to make a final disposition of

these sins in the lake of fire. Thus, so far as the work of atonement itself is concerned, the plan and work of mercy by which God's people are forgiven their sins, Satan has no part to act.—RH, July 3, 1883.

Christ as Sacrifice and Priest

About two years later Smith wrote about the twofold work of Christ as priest *and* sacrifice, and showed the difference between the two:

Remember that as antitype our Saviour acts in two capacities: First, he is antitype of the offerings: and, secondly, He is antitype of the priests. But He does not act in both capacities at the same time. His first work in connection with His ministry in the sanctuary was to offer Himself as a sacrifice, by dying on the cross. This He did once for all. In this act He was the antitype of all offerings for sin, both the individual offerings through the year, and the great offering on the day of atonement.

While suffering as a sacrifice, Christ was not acting as priest. But having by His crucifixion provided the effectual offering for all mankind, He was raised from the dead, and now ever liveth to intercede for men, and forgive the sins of all those who will seek such forgiveness through the merits of His blood. The virtue of His sacrifice continues, but He acts ever after His resurrection as priest, and not in any office typified by any animal.

Governed by this fact, it is impossible to understand the scapegoat as a type of Christ, as so many do. For, as we have seen, the scapegoat is not brought into action till the atonement in the most holy place is completed, which finishes the round of the sanctuary service, and then he is brought *alive* before the priest, and from his hands is forced to receive the load of the sins of the people, under which load, in charge of a fit man, he is sent away by the priest and away from both the priest and people to perish in the wilderness.—RH, March 10, 1885.

A Natural Order

W. H. Littlejohn, spoke of what he called "a natural order of events":

1. The slaying of the Lord's goat, which was fulfilled at the crucifixion; 2. The offering of the blood of the Lord's goat in the most holy place, that contained the ark, for the sins of the people, a work which will not be completed till Christ offers His blood on behalf of the last sinner who will be saved;* 3. The sending away of the scapegoat loaded with the sins of the people, into the wilderness, or a transaction that will not meet with its antitype until Christ has completed the work of atoning for the last sinner who will be saved."—RH, Sept. 9, 1884.

---

* Clearly Christ is not spilling literal blood; rather the language is symbolic.

THE TWO GOATS
Genesis, Revelation, and the Scapegoat

He also cited certain parallels evident in the book of Revelation:

"Scholars tell us that the Greek word translated 'bottomless pit' signifies an abyss, bottomless, deep, profound. It is the same word which is translated 'deep' in Genesis 1:2. In the sixteenth chapter of the Revelation there is an account of the seven last plagues, the closing one of which is poured out at the second advent. That plague, through the earthquakes that attend it, leaves the earth in a broken-down and desolate condition, resembling in a striking manner the situation in which it was at the time spoken of in Genesis 1:2. At that time, therefore, it would answer to the bottomless pit of Revelation 20:1-3. A wilderness in the Scriptures often means a barren, desolate, and uninhabited region, and would consequently very properly be employed to typify the earth without inhabitants and broken down in structure, as it will be after the coming of Christ. It is the earth in the chaotic condition just spoken of that I believe is the antitype of the wilderness into which the scapegoat was driven on the day of atonement."—*Ibid.*

Conditional and Absolute Pardon

In a following article, Littlejohn continued his study.

When the day of judgment is reached, Christ, our high priest, will offer before His Father His own blood for the purpose of making an atonement for the sins of His people. Then those sins will be pardoned absolutely, and Satan, the antitypical scapegoat, will have them rolled back upon his head. Previous to this time, confessing sinners had been pardoned conditionally, and the favor of God secured as the result of faith in Christ and the atonement to be perfected by Him in the future. All this while, however, the record of their sins was preserved; and in case they apostatized, they would be punished for those sins in the Judgment—agreeably to Ezekiel 18:24—as fully as if they had never repented of them.

This is in harmony with Hebrews 9:24-26, where we learn that Christ, unlike the high priest, was to enter into the most holy place but once to put away sin by the sacrifice of Himself: not, of course, by sacrificing Himself in the most holy place in the heavenly temple, but by presenting there in behalf of His people the blood that He shed for them on Calvary.

This is also in harmony with reason; for the plan that men should receive conditional pardon upon repentance, and absolute pardon if faithful, at the Judgment is much more consistent with wisdom than that their sins should be atoned for before they were committed and while they were still on probation.—RH, Sept. 16, 1884.

Accountability

Some months later Uriah Smith considered the matter of accountability for sin as portrayed in the Old Testament Day of

Atonement service:

> The removal of sin from the penitent by the death of the substituted victim did not cancel the sin iself, but only transferred it to some other object. The forgiveness, or removal, of the sin was relative, not absolute; that is, as related to the sinner, it was forgiven, it no longer stood against his account; but the sin itself was considered as still in existence, transferred to the sanctuary, and to be disposed of by other services yet to follow.
>
> Christ has done for us *in fact* what the ancient offering of animals did for the sinner *in figure;* that is, He has provided a medium in His own blood through which sin with its guilt may be removed from us, and transferred to some other party. Thus we can be saved; but our sins yet remain to be destroyed in some other vehicle.—RH, March 17, 1885. (Italics supplied.)

He illustrated responsibility for sin as follows:

> The practice of sin may therefore be fitly compared to a partnership business. In this business Satan is the senior partner; the sinner, the junior. The latter, having been brought into that relationship by deception and seduction, is granted the privilege, under certain conditions, of leaving the company, and retiring from the business with all its assets and its tremendous prospective liabilities.
>
> Upon whom, then, will these obligations fall? Upon the only remaining member of the firm, the instigator of the whole business, the senior partner, Satan. If the sinner chooses to maintain his partnership in that illegitimate business, he can do so and receive in his own person at last the terrible retribution that every sin must meet when it is purged out of existence by the fire of God.
>
> And this is what we are taught by the doctrine of the scapegoat. The penitent goes free, while Satan receives the sins he has incited him to commit, back upon his own head, to answer therefor in the settlement which he at last must meet.—*Ibid.*

Then he turned back to the symbol of the scapegoat:

> The antitypical scapegoat having thus received the load of sins from which the righteous have become free, and being confined to this desolate earth for a thousand years, is reserved to the day of perdition at the end of that period. This long cycle of years at length expires, and then appears the lake of fire prepared for the Devil and his angels. Into this fiery vortex they are plunged, and all the wicked in league with them are committed to the same doom. Then all the sins ever committed are punished, and in the persons of wicked human beings, evil angels, and Satan the father of all, they perish wholly and forever. Then the scapegoat has come to his end, and never is remembrance made of sin any more.—*Ibid.*

In Conclusion

The pioneers' view of the two goats used in the Day of

THE TWO GOATS

Atonement ritual differed from the general view of other Christians. Whereas the latter held both goats to symbolize the sacrifice of Christ, Smith and others argued cogently that the evidence called for a distinction between the two. The Lord's goat represented Christ; the scapegoat they identified as Satan.

In the scapegoat the pioneers saw an aspect of the sin problem not emphasized by their contemporary religious world: the resolution of the moral controversy and the assigning of sin to Satan, its originator and instigator. Also they regarded the prophecy of the binding of Satan, in Revelation 20, as the fulfillment of the symbolic banishment of the scapegoat to the wilderness.

The ritual of the two goats led the pioneers to perceive the nature of sin and the plan of salvation more broadly. The penitent sinner who brought his sin offering was fully forgiven, but they viewed his forgiveness as "conditional" or "relative." It did not imply that the penitent one thereafter stood in doubt of his forgiveness or lacked assurance of his acceptance until the Day of Atonement. Rather, it meant—with the sin transferred to the sanctuary—that ultimate accountability for it would be seen to by God. Beyond forgiveness based on the merits of Christ, symbolized in the sin offering, beyond the assumption of sin by the sanctuary, lay the day of retribution for Satan. That day of judgment would bring an end to sin and all its effects. Also it would reaffirm pardon for the believer who had chosen to remain faithful to Christ.

* * * *

Ellen White identifies Satan as the scapegoat in the following references:

Early Writings, pp. 178, 280, 281, 294, 295; *The Great Controversy*, pp. 422, 485, 658, 660, 673; *Prophets and Kings*, p. 591; *Patriarchs and Prophets*, p. 358; *Testimonies*, vol. 5, p. 475.

* * * *

ARTICLES QUOTED IN THIS CHAPTER

James White
   March 22, 1870, Our Faith and Hope—Removal of Sin (Series)

Uriah Smith
   March 18, 1858, Synopsis of the Present Truth (Series)
   July 3, 1883, Satan as the Scape-goat
   March 10, 1885, The Judgment of the Great Day (Series)
   March 17, 1885, The Judgment of the Great Day

J. H. Waggoner
   July 7, 1874, The Atonement

W. H. Littlejohn
   Sept. 9, 1884, The Temple in Heaven (Series)
   Sept. 16, 1884, The Temple in Heaven

10

Is the Adventist Position Biblical?

Earlier we noted what Uriah Smith said in 1874 when he responded to the charge that the Seventh-day Adventist Church derived its sanctuary doctrine from Ellen White. He reminded his readers that "works upon the sanctuary are among our standard publications. Hundreds of articles have been written upon the subject. But in no one of these are the visions once referred to as any authority on this subject, or the source from whence any view we hold has been derived. Nor does any preacher ever refer to them on this question. The appeal is invariably to the Bible, where there is abundant evidence for the views we hold on this subject."—RH, Dec. 22, 1874. Surely the reader who has followed this collection of statements from early Adventist writers will find Smith's substantiated.

The Sabbath Doctrine Developed

Another striking example of the relationship of visions to Bible study appeared in connection with when to begin and end the Sabbath.

Joseph Bates, an early advocate of the Sabbath, wrote a pamphlet on it in 1846 that came to the attention of James and Ellen White about the time of their marriage. They accepted the Sabbath as a result. Bates in his pamphlet argued for the beginning of the Sabbath at 6:00 P.M. Friday, applying Leviticus 23:32, which states that man should observe the day "from even to even."

Sabbath-observing Adventists, however, had differences of opinion. Some kept it as Bates advocated. Others began Sabbath observance at sunrise, sunset, or midnight. James White persuaded

J. N. Andrews to make a thorough study of the subject in 1855. Andrews presented his findings to the group. *After* his presentation, Ellen White received a vision that indicated he was correct.

Andrews' conclusions then appeared in the *Review and Herald* of December 4, 1855. He gave considerable attention to discrediting the six o'clock time advocated by Bates and accepted by several others, including Ellen White. Through a careful exposition of Scripture, he derived evidence for a sunset beginning time that settled the confusion. In a note following the article, he said, "In a short time I became entirely satisfied that the unanimous testimony of the Scriptures is that each day commences with the setting of the sun."—RH, Dec. 4, 1855.

James White commented on Andrews' article, saying that the author "decided to devote his time to the subject till he ascertained *what the Bible taught* in regard to it, and his article in this No. is the result of his investigations."—*Ibid.* (Italics supplied.)

Then White made the significant point: "Some have the impression that six o'clock time has been taught among us by the direct manifestation of the Holy Spirit [Ellen White's visions]. This is a mistake. 'From even to even' was the teaching, from which six o'clock time has been inferred. We now rejoice that Brother Andrews has presented *the Bible testimony* on this question in his accustomed forcible, candid manner, which settles the question beyond all doubt that the Sabbath commences not only at even, but at the setting of the sun."—*Ibid.* (Italics supplied.)

Speaking of her vision following Andrews' presentation, Ellen White explained, "I saw that it is even so, 'From even unto even, shall ye celebrate your sabbath.' Said the angel, 'Take the Word of God, read it, understand, and ye cannot err. Read carefully, and ye shall there find *what* even is, and *when* it is.'

"I asked the angel if the frown of God had been upon His people for commencing the Sabbath as they had. I was directed back to the first rise of the Sabbath, and followed the people of God up to this time, but did not see that the Lord was displeased, or frowned upon them. I inquired why it had been thus, that at this late day we must change the time of commencing the Sabbath.

"Said the angel, 'Ye shall understand, but not yet, not yet.' Said the angel, 'If light come, and that light is set aside or rejected, then comes condemnation and the frown of God; but before the light comes, there is no sin, for there is not light for them to reject.' "—*Testimonies*, vol. 1, p. 116 (November, 1855).

Some years later, James White recalled the whole experience:

The question naturally arises. If the visions are given to correct the erring, why did she [Mrs. White] not sooner see the error of the six o'clock time? For one, I have ever been thankful that God corrected the error in His own good time, and did not suffer an unhappy division to exist among us upon the point. But, dear reader, the work of the Lord upon this point is in perfect harmony with His manifestations to us on others, and in harmony with the correct position upon spiritual gifts.

It does not appear to be the desire of the Lord to teach His people by the gifts of the Spirit on the Bible questions until His servants have diligently searched His Word. When this was done upon the subject of time to commence the Sabbath, and most were established, and some were in danger of being out of harmony with the body on this subject, then, yes, *then* was the very time for God to magnify His goodness in the manifestation of the gift of His Spirit in the accomplishment of its proper work.

The Sacred Scriptures are given us as the rule of faith and duty, and we are commanded to search them. If we fail to understand and fully obey the truths in consequence of not searching the Scriptures as we should, or a want of consecration and spiritual discernment, and God in mercy in His own time corrects us by some manifestation of the gifts of His Holy Spirit, instead of murmuring that He did not do it before, let us humbly acknowledge His mercy, and praise Him for His infinite goodness in condescending to correct us all.

Let the gifts have their proper place in the church. God has never set them in the very front, and commanded us to look to them to lead us in the path of truth, and the way to Heaven. His Word He has magnified. The Scriptures of the Old and New Testament are man's lamp to light up his path to the kingdom. Follow that, but if you err from Bible truth, and are in danger of being lost, it may be that God will in the time of His choice correct you, and bring you back to the Bible and save you.—RH, Feb. 25, 1868.

The Bible as Final Word

J. N. Andrews illustrated the Bible-centered approach of the pioneers in their study on the sanctuary when he wrote in 1874:

The Bible doctrine of the sanctuary is this: That the sanctuary is the place where the high priest stands to offer blood before God for the sins of those who come to God through Him. The central object in the sanctuary is the ark which contains the law of God that man has broken. The cover of this ark was called the mercy seat, because mercy came to those who had broken the law beneath it, when the high priest sprinkled the blood of sin offering upon it, provided they accompanied his work by repentance and faith. Last of all was the work of cleansing the sanctuary when the high priest by blood removed the sins of the people from the sanctuary into which they had been borne by the ministration of the priests before God.

We now invite attention to the testimony of the Bible respecting the sanctuary.

IS THE ADVENTIST POSITION BIBLICAL?

1. There are two covenants; the first, or old covenant, extends from the time of Moses to the death of Christ; the second, or new covenant, begins at the death of Christ and extends forward to the consummation. Gal. 4:24-26; Heb. 8:7-13; Luke 22:20.

2. The first covenant had a sanctuary which was the tabernacle erected by Moses. Heb. 9:1-7.

3. The new covenant has a sanctuary which is the temple of God in Heaven, into which our High Priest entered when He ascended up on high. Heb. 8:1-5.

4. When Moses erected the tabernacle, he was commanded by God to make it according to the pattern which He showed to him; and this pattern must have been a representation of the temple of God in Heaven, for the earthly sanctuary is declared to be a pattern of the heavenly. Ex. 25:9, 40; Heb. 8:5; 9:23.

5. The earthly sanctuary consisted of two holy places; the first of which contained the table of shewbread, the candlestick with seven lamps, and the golden altar of incense; and the second contained the ark of God's testament with the tables on which the ten commandments were written by the finger of God, and over which was the mercy seat with the cherubim of glory overshadowing it. Ex. 40:18-28; Heb. 9:1-5.

6. The temple of God in Heaven is not only spoken of as the original from which the earthly sanctuary was copied (Heb. 9:23, 24; 1 Chron. 28:11, 12, 19), but it is also spoken of as consisting of holy places, in the plural. See Hebrews 8:2; 9:8, 12, 24; 10:19, in each of which verses the original is holy places, in the plural, and they are so rendered in various translations.

The word sanctuary in the Bible, except in the few cases where it is used figuratively, refers always to the place where the high priest ministers before God for the sins of the people. It was first the tabernacle erected by Moses; then it was the temple built by Solomon, which was a more glorious structure than the tabernacle, but with the same two holy places; and when the typical sacrifices ended in the death of Christ, who is the true sin offering, the earthly sanctuary, or holy places, ceased to be the center of God's worship, and Christ entered the temple in heaven as a great High Priest—the minister of the sanctuary and of the true tabernacle which the Lord pitched, and not man.—RH, March 10, 1874.

A Bible Study

For convenience we include a Bible study that appeared in the *Review* before the turn of the century. It summarized the scriptural basis for the Adventist belief regarding the sanctuary:

1. What did the angel say to Daniel? Dan. 8:14.
2. Where was God's sanctuary in the old dispensation? Ps. 102:19.
3. Where is it in this dispensation? Heb. 8:1, 2.
4. What did God tell Moses to do? Ex. 25:8.

THE SANCTUARY, 1844, AND THE PIONEERS

5. How did Moses know how to make it? Ex. 25:8, 9, 40; Heb. 8:5; 9:23.

6. Give a description of the sanctuary that Moses made. Heb. 9:1-5; Ex. 26:33.

7. Are there two places in the heavenly sanctuary? Heb. 9:24. Then if the *places* made with hands are the *figures* of the heavenly, there must be two places there.

8. How many under priests assisted in the earthly sanctuary? 1 Chron. 24:4, 5.

9. Is this order recognized in the heavenly sanctuary? Rev. 4:4, 5. In Smith's *Bible Dictionary* the term "priest" is thus defined: "The English word is derived from the Greek *presbyter* signifying an elder."

10. Were these elders recognized as priests? Rev. 5:8-10.

11. Were there seven golden candlesticks in the earthly sanctuary? Heb. 9:2; Ex. 25:37.

12. What else did Moses make? And where did the he place it? Ex. 30:1; 40:26, 27.

13. Do we find the same in the heavenly sanctuary? Rev. 4:5; 8:3; 9:13.

14. Moses made an ark also; where did he place it? Ex. 25:10, 11; 17:18-20; 26:33, 34.

15. What was the ark called, and why? Ex. 26:33; 25:16, 21.

16. Is the ark of which this was a pattern in heaven? Rev. 15:5; 11:19.

17. Is the same language used in speaking of the ark in both sanctuaries? (Compare Rev. 15:5 with Num. 9:15.)

18. What did God want Moses to build a sanctuary for? Ex. 25:8.

19. In the earthly sanctuary where did God dwell by the symbol of His presence? Ex. 25:22.

20. Where is God's throne in heaven? Ps. 99:1. Christ is set down on the right hand of the throne of the Majesty in the heavens, and is a Minister, or Priest, of the sanctuary in heaven. Heb. 8:1-4. Then the throne of God is in the sanctuary in heaven, and John was looking into the heavenly sanctuary when he saw the seven lamps of fire, the altar of incense, and the ark of the testimony.

21. What was the testimony that Moses put into the ark? Ex. 31:18; Deut. 10:3-5.

22. Did God have a law before the tables of the law were given to Moses? Gen. 26:5; Ex. 13:9; 16:4; 18:16.

23. How long after the manna was given in Exodus 16:4, before the law was spoken from Sinai? Ex. 12:2, 3, 9, 10; 16:1; 19:1, 15, 16; 15:24-26. One month and two days before the law was formally proclaimed from Sinai, the manna was given to prove them if they would walk in God's law. Now that we have found that God had a law before He spoke it from Sinai, we must conclude that the law given to Moses on tables of stone was only a copy, or pattern, of the law of God in heaven. As the ark in the earthly sanctuary was called the ark of the testimony because it contained the copy of God's law given to Moses, so the ark in the heavenly sanctuary is called the ark of the testimony, because it contains the law of God.

24. In the earthly sanctuary, did the priests minister in both

apartments? Heb. 9:6, 7.

25. What was the daily sacrifice in the first apartment? Ex. 29:38, 39, 42.

26. What was the manner of transferring the sin from the sinner to the sanctuary, and securing his forgiveness? Lev. 4:27-30; 4:14-18; 5:5-9; 10:16-18.

27. What were the services in the second apartment? Lev. 16:29, 30, 33.

28. What was the manner of removing the sin from the earthly sanctuary? Lev. 16:5-22. The service of the priest in the earthly sanctuary represented the service in the heavenly. Heb. 8:4, 5; 7:21-27.

29. Both the earthly and the heavenly sanctuary are cleansed with blood. Heb. 9:22-24, 12.

30. We are told that the sins of God's people will be blotted out. Isa. 43:25.

31. When will this be done? Acts 3:19-21. The time of the restitution of all things is when Christ comes the second time to this earth, and restores to His people what was lost through sin: Purity (Col. 1:13, 14); Life (Rom. 8:23; John 5:28, 29); The dominion (Micah 4:8).—RH, Nov. 14, 1893.

The obvious answer to the question as to whether our position is Biblical has been repeatedly demonstrated throughout this study. We have always held that the Bible is the source of our doctrines. It is true regarding the sanctuary belief as well as all others.

* * * *

ARTICLES QUOTED IN THIS CHAPTER

J. N. Andrews
    March 10, 1874, The Sanctuary of the Bible

Uriah Smith
    Dec. 22, 1874, The Sanctuary

Bible Study
    Nov. 14, 1893, Sanctuary

James White
    Feb. 25, 1868, Commencement of the Sabbath

11

Historical Reminiscing

Seventh-day Adventists have important reasons to be forward looking. We preach a message designed to prepare a people for the second coming of Christ. But we also need to be conscious of the present, because we realize that a judgment is going on *at this time* in heaven's sanctuary. We believe that when that judgment concludes, the world's probation will close forever. That fact adds a sobering aspect to what we proclaim.

But we are never to forget our past. The prophetic voice in our midst has made that point clear. "We have nothing to fear for the future, except as we shall forget the way the Lord has led us, and His teaching in our past history."—*Life Sketches*, p. 196.

James White Looks Back

James White had the highest respect for the best-known leader of the Advent movement in America—William Miller. He wrote that "William Miller gave the best light he then had on the Sanctuary and its cleansing" (RH, April 18, 1854).

J. N. Andrews Looks Back

J. N. Andrews spoke of the importance of the doctrine. "The Seventh-day Adventists have a definite position on the subject of the Sanctuary. In this thing there is a striking contrast between them and all other Advent bodies, who, on this question, are in a state of complete confusion. Now this fact is not a little remarkable. For if we go back to the time when the great disappointment threw the whole Advent body into perplexity, we shall find that that disappointment arose from the view then prevalent among them concerning the Sanctuary. The S.D. Adventists, having carefully reviewed the whole ground, have a definite position to offer which they consider a complete explanation of the subject.

"Moreover, the view that they have to present of the Sanctuary subject is the great central doctrine in their system; for it inseparably connects all the points in their faith, and presents the subject as one grand whole."—RH, Oct. 18, 1864.

Uriah Smith Looks Back

Uriah Smith saw the importance of every member having a knowledge of the doctrine. "The subject of the sanctuary is one which should specially engage the attention of S.D. Adventists. It is a subject peculiar to this people. There is no other denomination whose views on this question correspond with, or even approximate, the views set forth in the works issued from this Office. Every one of our people should therefore make it a point of first importance to become thoroughly conversant with this subject."—RH, Feb. 20, 1883.

He expressed amazement that the sanctuary doctrine had remained undiscovered for so long. "Looking at the subject in a general sense, that which is perhaps most calculated to excite our wonder is the fact that a question so intimately connected with, and so essentially modifying, some of the most important subjects of the Bible, should have lain so long unnoticed. And this furnishes all the greater reason why, now that the light is shining upon it, and its commanding position in the great temple of truth is discovered, the most earnest efforts should be made to bring it to the attention of the people.

"This subject is intimately connected with the prophecies, and this may be one reason why it has not sooner engaged the special attention of Bible students; for it has been reserved to this present generation, living in 'the time of the end,' to behold the seal broken from the prophetic page and to see a wonderful increase of knowledge respecting its soul-inspiring utterances."—*Ibid.*

Washington Morse Looks Back

Washington Morse experienced the 1844 disappointment and went through a period of discouragement for some time afterward. But writing in retrospect of Adventist beginnings, he presented one of the most interesting and deeply moving accounts of any participant:

"And he said unto me, Unto two thousand and three hundred

days; then shall the sanctuary be cleansed." Dan. 8:14.

Much ink has been spent in commenting on this text. Perhaps there is not another verse in the Bible that has been so widely discussed as this one, and perhaps no other passage has proved, and will prove, the downfall of so many nations who reject its plain teachings. The Saviour pronounced the most severe woe upon the Jews, because they knew not the "time" of their visitation.

That time was the seventy weeks of Daniel 9:24, cut off from the two thousand three hundred days, or years, and was the first four hundred and ninety years of that period. As we came down to that generation where is seen the end of the longest prophetic period in the Bible, and the only one for which we have a Bible date, God, through His servants, sent forth the message of Revelation 14:6, 7, announcing, "The hour of his judgment *is come.*" The *time* was the moving principle. It was a searching test to those living in that generation.

I was permitted to take part in that blessed work from its beginning. In great power God set His seal to it by His Holy Spirit. The doors of the churches were thrown open for Brother Miller and others to preach the coming of Christ; and thus when this truth was preached, a great harvest of converts was added to the churches. This work continued until January 1, 1844. At that time a change took place, as the majority believed that the prophetic periods all ended there. From that time until spring, we had no freedom nor liberty with our former brethren in the churches to which we belonged. But we understood that the twenty-three hundred days did not end until the spring of 1844; and it was with great solemnity that we came to that period.

Some of our brethren could not go forward, and put in their crops, while others did so reluctantly. We felt sure our reckoning was correct, and that the Saviour would come at that time. While standing in that waiting position, the light of the second angel's message flashed upon us; and a voice came like a rushing mighty wind, "Come out of her, my people." No one knew who raised the cry first; but as we heard from our brethren north, south, east, and west, all had the same experience, and immediately left their respective churches. Yes, and we all left our *creeds*, or what had before been our differences. Right there we formed the Philadelphian state of the church—a church of *brotherly love.*

Probably from sixty to one hundred thousand persons came out from the Protestant churches within a month; and O, how God blessed this act! Right there we ran out of all our published time, and practically went to sleep on *time*, according to Matthew 25:5. This we saw was the *tarrying time.* We read, "Though it [the vision] tarry, wait for it." In this position we continued until about the middle of July, 1844. Here we discovered a discrepancy in our reckoning, and found that the decree of Artaxerxes for the restoration of Jerusalem, which formed the starting point for the twenty-three hundred days, went into effect in the *autumn* of the year B.C. 457, and not at the beginning of the year, as had been formerly believed. Reckoning from the autumn of 457, the twenty-three hundred years terminated in the autumn of 1844.

Arguments drawn from the Old Testament types also pointed to that autumn as the time when the event represented by the cleansing of the sanctuary must take place. Under the Mosaic system the cleansing of the sanctuary, or the great day of atonement, occurred on the tenth day of the Jewish seventh month, when the high priest, having made an atonement for all Israel, and thus removed their sins from the sanctuary, came forth and blessed the people. So it was believed that Christ, our great High Priest, would appear to purify the earth by the destruction of sin and sinners, and to bless His waiting people with immortality, on the tenth day of the seventh month, the great day of atonement—the time of the cleansing of the sanctuary—which in the year 1844 fell on the 22d of October.

This was regarded as the time of the Lord's coming. This position was in harmony with the proofs already presented that the twenty-three hundred days would terminate in the autumn, and the conclusion seemed irresistible. In the parable of Matthew 25, the time of waiting and slumber is followed by the coming of the bridegroom. This was in accordance with the arguments just presented, both from prophecy and from the types. They carried strong conviction of their truthfulness, and the "midnight cry" was heralded by thousands of believers. It went from city to city, from village to village, and into remote country places.

None knew where it started. It arose *simultaneously*. There was fervent prayer and unreserved consecration to God. At the call, "Behold, the Bridegroom cometh; go ye out to meet him," we *all* arose and trimmed our lamps. We studied the Word of God with greater interest than we ever had studied it. It was not the most talented, but the most *humble* and *devoted*, who were to hear and obey the call. Farmers left their crops standing in the fields, mechanics laid down their tools, merchants left their merchandise; and all went forth with tears and rejoicing to give the warning. Here is where the "midnight cry" came in to give power to the second message. Those who had formerly led out in the cause were among the last to give the warning.

As *time* was the moving principle, we did proclaim, with all that positiveness brought to view in Revelation 10:5, 6, that time should be no longer. We had no "ifs" in our faith: we believed God's Word just as He designed we should. If we had seen the third angel's message then, we could not have given the first angel's message. We gave up the world, with all its pleasures and charms—our property, our reputation, our all. No one whose faith was genuine could do any other way. The world saw that we believed just what we preached. We gave it all; yes, we consecrated all we had and were, to God. We were the happiest people that ever lived this side of the apostolic days.—RH, March 7, 1899.

Morse drew an important conclusion:

It is through the light upon the sanctuary question that we know and understand the work of the judgment that has been going on in heaven since the end of the twenty-three hundred years of Daniel 8:14. And as we near the time when the cases of the living will come up, there will be a corresponding work going forward upon earth. Hence this is a time of supreme importance to every living soul. We do not know just when our names will be called. Now is the time for us to be free from sin, let Jesus have the whole heart, make no reserve. We are to be like "men that *wait* for their lord, when he will return from the wedding." Luke 12:36. No one can be said to *wait* until He is *ready*. Now is the time to watch, lest coming to our cases suddenly, He find us not prepared.—*Ibid.*

S. N. Haskell Looks Back

A Fall Council at Lincoln, Nebraska, in 1904 asked S. N. Haskell to review early Adventist history. He had joined the movement in 1853, so he could remember back nearly to the beginning. The following excerpt comes from his sermon delivered on September 17, 1904, almost exactly sixty years after the Disappointment:

> When the time passed in 1844, there were none who believed the truth as we now hold it. All believed the prophecies that brought us to that time. Then began a greater searching of the Bible than had ever been, probably, at any time since the days of the apostles. They went over and over the old arguments concerning the prophecies that pointed to 1844, and after most thorough examination they could see no other conclusion than that the prophetic periods terminated at that time.—RH, Oct. 27, 1904.

Haskell noted the importance of reviewing the past:

> I will call your attention to the eighth and ninth chapters of Daniel. The application of the prophecy contained in these two chapters at one time stirred the world. They were the basis of the preaching of Joseph Wolf in Asia and Europe and in the islands of the sea, of Edward Irving in England, of William Miller in America, and of others who led out in different parts of the world. Unknown to one another, these men preached the central truth that made a separate and distinct people. The truths which they presented from the prophecies of the eighth and ninth chapters of Daniel have been lost sight of to a certain extent. I have been told by some that they had been taught that we no longer need these prophecies; we need simply faith in Christ.
>
> Now, my friends, let us see if we do not need these prophecies. When Moses brought Israel out from the land of Egypt, his last work was to recount the dealings of God with His people. About six years before Jerusalem was destroyed, Paul wrote to the Hebrews not to cast away their confidence, but to remember the days when they were illuminated—to learn the history of the past, and to "call to remembrance the former days, in which, after ye were illuminated, ye endured a great fight of afflictions."

HISTORICAL REMINISCING

And so it has been again and again. When God has raised up a people, and they have lost the spirit of the message that made them a distinct people, He has called upon them to review the past.—*Ibid.*

Haskell's sermon continued:

I suppose that the time argument was studied over by the disappointed ones more than ten thousand times to see where the mistake was, and it came out 1844 every time. Why did they think the Lord would come in 1844? They reasoned that the sanctuary was the earth, and the cleansing of the sanctuary, the cleansing of the earth; that the earth would be cleansed by fire, and the cleansing would take place at the coming of the Lord. They made the text read, Unto two thousand and three hundred days, or years, then shall the Lord come; and they believed it.

Did you ever hear people laugh about it, and say that men back there sold their farms? I have heard them say so, and that they would not be such fools as that. The only question is whether if they really believed it, they would *act* as if they did. The believers did sell their farms, and left their crops unharvested in the fields. One man in New Hampshire, Leonard Hastings, said, "I thought the Lord would come in the autumn of 1844, and I did not dig my potatoes. The neighbors talked about putting a guardian over me, but they finally concluded that as I was comparatively an old man and good citizen, it would be a disgrace, so they did not do it. That year the potatoes rotted in the cellars, and my neighbors who dug their potatoes lost them. But I waited until the time had passed, and the potatoes in the ground were all sound, and I had potatoes to sell to the very ones who were going to put a guardian over me."—RH, Nov. 3, 1904.

Speaking of the study of Scripture by early Adventist pioneers, Haskell concluded:

They were careful not to introduce anything that had not a solid foundation in the Bible. They were laying the foundation for the structure of a faith that would gather souls from every part of the earth. God gave them a spirit of carefulness that they might not weave into the structure any error. We have never had to renounce one position thus taken.—*Ibid.*

At the beginning of our study we observed that history has repeated itself many times with regard to opposition to the Adventist teaching on the sanctuary and its cleansing. Certain objections have again and again come up against the doctrine. We conclude with one such challenge in 1887, nearly one hundred years ago. We have already met J. W. Morton, but some further background on him may be of interest.

The Story of J. W. Morton

J. W. Morton began his public ministry in the Reformed

Presbyterian Church. He traveled to Haiti as a missionary for that denomination in 1847. But study on the subject of Sabbathkeeping led him to return to the United States in 1849, where he defended his belief in the seventh-day Sabbath in a church trial. Dropped from the Presbyterian clergy as a result, he became a Seventh Day Baptist minister and served that church until his death in 1893 at the age of 72.

He contributed to the Seventh Day Baptist Church in a variety of ways, earning the reputation of "an able writer, a fine scholar, and a consecrated Christian man and minister of the gospel" (*Seventh-day Baptists in Europe and America*, 1910, p. 398). Morton held positions as pastor, school administrator, evangelist, editor, translator of the New Testament from Greek to English, professor of Latin and Greek, and author.

His writing on the Sabbath doctrine especially interested Seventh-day Adventists. One of his tracts, a study titled *Vindication of the True Sabbath*, Seventh Day Baptists first published in 1850, shortly after he joined their church. Our publishing house in Battle Creek obtained permission to print three editions of his sixty-eight-page tract in 1860, 1868, and 1872.

It appears, however, that Morton did not in later years, at least, have positive relations with Adventists. Writing in the Seventh Day Baptist journal *The Sabbath Recorder*, on July 21, 1887, he launched a strong attack on the sanctuary and the investigative judgment beliefs. Because of the nature of his presentation, Uriah Smith felt compelled to respond, and did so immediately in an article in the *Review and Herald.* He systematically dealt with several points made by Morton. (Numbers refer to Morton's comments. The heart of Smith's reply follows each.)

> 1. He admits that there is a sanctuary in heaven, but claims that it has but one apartment, and that is the "most holy place."
>
> *   *   *   *
>
> To this it is sufficient to reply that the earthly was a type of the heavenly, and the "pattern" according to which Moses was commanded to make the earthly, was the heavenly Sanctuary itself. Working after that pattern, Moses made a sanctuary with two apartments, a holy place and a most holy place. . . .
>
> 2. Mr. M. will have Christ perform no service above, except in the most holy place. He says: "The services performed by the priests in the court of the tabernacle and in the first tabernacle itself were all typical of the work of Christ on earth, and were completely fulfilled when He expired on the cross."

* * * *

According to this, Christ must have performed a portion of His priesthood on earth; but this directly contradicts the apostle Paul, who declares positively that He accomplishes no part of His priestly work here below. In Hebrews 8:4, 5, he says: "For if he were on earth, *he should not be a priest*, seeing that there are priests that offer gifts according to the law; who serve unto the example and shadow of heavenly things." . . .

3. He has Christ make the atonement immediately on His ascension to heaven. He says: "In the natural order of things, the atonement preceded the session of Christ on the mediatorial throne. . . . His very first act, therefore, after His ascension, was to present His atoning blood in the holy of holies. There He sat down by the Father's side." . . .

* * * *

What he lays down as the "natural order" every reader of the Old Testament knows is exactly the reverse of the natural order; for in that yearly round of priestly service which prefigured the work of Christ in heaven, making the atonement was the *closing up* of the work, not the *beginning* of it; it was the *last* act, not the *first*. . . .

4. He falls into the usual chaos over Hebrews 10:20. Verses 19 and 20 read as follows: "Having therefore, brethren, boldness to enter into the holiest by the blood of Jesus, by a new and living way, which he hath consecrated for us, through the vail, that is to say, his flesh." In reference to this, Mr. M. comments as follows:

"The vail therefore was an essential part of the earthly sanctuary. This vail represented Christ's human nature—His flesh. Heb. 10:20. When this human nature was lacerated on the cross, and He was in the agonies of death, 'the vail of the temple was rent in twain.' The mortal flesh was thenceforward to be replaced by the glorified and immortal body, in which the worshiper might approach into the presence of God." . . .

* * * *

According to the view here set forth, it seems that "Christ's human nature" was shown to Moses, and he was commanded to make something to represent it; and the nearest likeness he could devise was a curtain of fine linen, wrought all over with figures of cherubim suspended before the most holy place of the sanctuary! . . .

But a slight transposition will free the text from all ambiguity, and make the apostle's meaning clear and consistent. Thus: "Having, therefore, brethren, boldness to enter through the vail into the holiest by the blood of Jesus, by a new and living way, that is to say, His flesh, which He hath consecrated for us." Thus it appears that Christ's "flesh," that is, the offering which He has provided, is—not the vail, but the new and living way by which we enter through the vail into the Sanctuary on high, and have access to the one Mediator between God and man.

5. To prove that there is but one apartment in the heavenly

Sanctuary, Mr. M. quotes those texts in Hebrews which speak about the "holy place," as it is rendered in the common version. Thus Hebrews 9:8: "The Holy Ghost this signifying, that the way into the holiest of all [or, Revised Version, holy place] was not yet made manifest, while as the first tabernacle was yet standing." Verse 12: "Entered in once into the holy place." Hebrews 10:19: "Having therefore, brethren, boldness to enter into the holiest by the blood of Jesus." And, following the Revised Version, he quotes Hebrews 9:24 as follows: "For Christ entered not into a holy place made with hands, like in pattern to the true."

* * * *

Now. Mr. M. knows better than to quote these texts thus, and make this application of them. He is a Greek scholar, and well understands that in every one of these instances the word is in the original in the plural number, reading "holy places," and should be so translated. . . .

6. Speaking of S.D. Adventists, he further says: "They teach that when Jesus *did* enter into the holy place, it was not for the purpose of presenting His blood, and thus making an atonement, for the sins of His people, but rather that He might enter upon what they call 'The Investigative Judgment,' for the purpose of ascertaining from the books of God's remembrance the actual moral and spiritual condition and character of those who in all ages have professed to be His people."

* * * *

We are utterly unable to account for such a statement as this; for by the insertion of the word "not," which should not be there, it expresses exactly the reverse of the truth. The very thing we do teach, as every reader of our literature knows, is that Christ entered the most holy place for the very purpose of presenting His blood, and making an atonement for His people. . . .

7. He speaks of us as "the self-styled 'Remnant Church.'". . .

* * * *

The Bible calls the last generation of Christians, those who will be living at the second coming of Christ, "the *remnant* of the woman's seed." Rev. 12:17. Now whether there is such a body on the earth today or not, all depends on the question whether or not we have reached the last days and Christ is about to appear. If we have reached that time, as we suppose, there is a "remnant" of those who have constituted the church, now on earth. And whenever that time comes, all who are ready for Christ's coming will belong to that "remnant." Even Seventh-day Baptists, if they are saved, must help compose it. We really do not see the call for the sneers with which he interlards his essay on this point.

8. He says that the 2,300 days are literal days, and that the prophecy has been fulfilled, and that if he knew more of history he could tell where.

HISTORICAL REMINISCING

* * * *

It will be enough if the reader will consider what a wonderful literal prophecy, on this ground, this would be. Twenty-three hundred literal days are not quite six and a half years. And when the angel propounded the momentous inquiry, "How long shall be the vision . . . to give both the Sanctuary and the host to be trodden under foot?" how sublime would be the answer, would it not, "Unto six years and a quarter; then shall the Sanctuary be cleansed"? He admits that in Numbers 13:34 and Ezekiel 4:4-6 days represent years, yet cannot see how in the symbolic prophecy of Daniel 8:14, days can also represent years.

* * * *

He says: "I am perfectly satisfied, on the contrary, that there is not a single passage in God's word in which it is clear from the context that this word [day] has any such meaning [day for a year]."

* * * *

Has he ever read Daniel 9:25? Here a period of sixty-nine weeks is marked off, to reach from the commandment to restore and build Jerusalem to the Messiah the Prince. All expositors, except Jewish, understand this to refer to the revelation of Christ at His first advent. In sixty-nine weeks there are 483 days. Were these days literal, or do they represent years? It would be the merest quibble to object that the word "days" is not here used. No one can deny that the same principle is here involved. If the time is literal, it is 483 literal days. If it is symbolic, it is 483 years. According to Mr. M. it must be literal. But who supposes that a prophecy was given covering only sixty-nine literal weeks—about a year and a third—before the manifestation of Christ as the Messiah the Prince? Or who supposes that a commandment to restore Jerusalem went forth a year and a third before Christ came? The idea is too absurd to mention. But if the days in Daniel 9 are symbolic, a day for a year, the days in Daniel 8, which Daniel 9 is given to explain, are also symbolic.

10. We now come to the crushing climax of his whole effort. He says: "What I have written above respecting the teachings of the self-styled 'Remnant Church,' I have written in all sincerity and good will, but with very little hope that any member of that body will be influenced thereby. I know full well that though the doctrines criticized above are diametrically opposed to the Bible, they are in perfect accord with the teachings of their prophetess, whose so-called relations [revelations?] are permanent with those who believe in her inspiration. If the apostles contradict her 'visions' and 'testimonies,' so much the worse for the apostles! But I do most earnestly entreat those of God's dear people who still believe in the Bible, *and the Bible alone*, as the rule of faith and manners, to pause and weigh the matter carefully before plunging into this miry pool of human invention."

* * * *

We are sorry Mr. Morton could not finish his essay without unveiling to public view a darkened chamber of his soul out of whose murky recesses the serpent of falsehood thrusts its head to hiss, and the blind owl of bigotry and prejudice lifts up its voice to hoot. If he has investigated the subject at all, he knows that the views we hold on the question of the Sanctuary were not suggested by any vision from Sister White, and in all our investigations of the subject we never appeal to any of her writings, but rest the argument wholly upon the Scriptures, taking the ground on this, as upon all other subjects, that whatever is not sustained by the Bible must fall. But he must have his fling at the "prophetess," even though it be at the expense of truth; he must endeavor to raise prejudice against us, by representing that we would deliberately set aside a positive statement of the apostles, in behalf of a vision or testimony from Sister White.—RH, Aug. 2, 1887.

Morton answered Smith's article a few months later:

This doctrine of the "investigative judgment," as taught by the "remnant church," which, at best, rests upon an uncertain and improbable interpretation of Daniel 7:9, 10, gives the lie to Jesus, to John, to Paul, and to Peter. Is it any wonder that evangelical Christians should hold it in abomination? It is not only unscriptural, it is equally unphilosophical and unworthy of the well-known character of God. The thought that a God of infinite justice and fair dealing would, by a sort of "star-chamber" process, judge and sentence to utter destruction millions of His own creatures, without a hearing, is the very *quintessence* of absurdity. It is little short of blasphemy. I know of no more truth-denying, God-dishonoring doctrine in the whole range of modern theology. This is my deliberate testimony.—Quoted by Smith in RH, May 22, 1888.

Smith's reply:

Mr. M. is still confused with the old "medieval" idea of the judgment, which ignores all order and regularity in the work, but has the whole human family come up in one indiscriminate, conglomerate mass, and one by one receive their examination and sentence. How much time would this occupy? Take, for example, the lowest computation of the present generation, 1,400,000,000, and give to the judgment of each person one minute, which would certainly be short enough time, would it not? and how long would it take to judge just this one generation? Reducing the number to hours, days, and years, omitting fractions, we have 23,333,333 hours, 972,222 days, 2,663 years. That is, it would take over two and one-half thousand years to go through the present generation, according to Mr. M's "orthodox" view, and gather out those who are to be made immortal at Christ's coming, and which Paul declares is accomplished "in the twinkling of an eye," at the sound of the trumpet.—*Ibid.*

In response to Morton's "star-chamber" charge, Smith said:

But the most singular part of his criticism is that he accuses God of pursuing a sort of "star-chamber" process unless he gives all the wicked "a hearing" at the judgment. A hearing, indeed! What kind of a hearing does he suppose the wicked are entitled to, or will be accorded to them? Will they be permitted to come up and deny the crimes recorded against them, or charge the heavenly records with partial or exaggerated statements, or urge palliating circumstances in extenuation of their evil deeds? What other evidence could come in to influence the findings of the court, when they have before them the complete life record of the culprit with every thought, motive, purpose, and secret thing—the whole character photographed upon the page of destiny exactly as it is? Can a person have any further "hearing" than this? Cannot the court make up a just sentence from all this, and justly bring the doomed man up afterward to hear that sentence? The question answers itself.

The sins of the righteous are blotted out before Christ comes bringing with Him the reward of immortality for them, or both Peter and Paul have testified incorrectly, and there is no lesson to be learned from type and antitype. And the wicked have their sentence prepared in the judgment of the thousand years, for so John states, in Revelation 20:4.—*Ibid.*

Smith concluded:

At the end of the thousand years, for the first and last and only time, the whole human family are together before the throne: the righteous in the city, the wicked outside. Luke 13:28; Rev. 20:9. There sentence is pronounced upon the wicked, the executed; and in that sentence they "give account" of their idle words, and "answer" for all their abominable deeds. Then the King pronounces the great blessing upon the righteous, and invites them to take possession of the renewed and purified earth, the kingdom prepared for them from the foundation of the world, which they are to possess forever and ever.

With a rational, consistent view of this subject, the testimony of the whole Bible comes together in the completest harmony.—*Ibid.*

* * * *

ARTICLES QUOTED IN THIS CHAPTER

James White
    April 18, 1854, The Twenty-three Hundred Days

J. N. Andrews
    Oct. 18, 1864, The Sanctuary

Uriah Smith
    Feb. 20, 1883, The Sanctuary
    Aug. 2, 1887, J. W. Morton and the Sanctuary Question
    May 22, 1888, The Investigative Judgment

Washington Morse
    March 7, 1899, The Cleansing of the Sanctuary

S. N. Haskell
    Oct. 27, 1904, The Sanctuary
    Nov. 3, 1904, The Sanctuary

A Concluding Statement

For some centuries after Christ lived on earth, the Christian church experienced a worldwide growth nothing short of phenomenal. Even persecution contributed to it. But gradually spiritual darkness settled over the religious world. Hundreds of years of such conditions became known as the Dark Ages. Bibles were scarce and existed in languages not understood by the average person.

Then came the invention of movable type and the printing press. The Protestant Reformation quickly followed. Reformers translated the Bible into the common languages, and the printing press made it more available to everyone. The Reformers also proclaimed the message that human priests were not mankind's exclusive intercessors. "Every person is a priest," they said, with the privilege of praying to God directly.

The Christian world, including Seventh-day Adventists, faces a different situation today. The Bible is widely available in every major language and in scores of versions. But some still imply that the common people cannot really understand the Bible. They claim that a person needs to know the original languages or the historical context, or that there is only one method of study or interpretation that one can use. That only the scholar or some special group can understand or interpret Bible truth. And there may be some Seventh-day Adventists who believe that no scripture can be understood without the aid of Ellen White.

But understanding is for the child or the simple, as well as the adult or the highly educated. I am not suggesting that it is preferable to be ignorant. We should study earnestly, seeking to know all we can. But we are to let the Bible speak to us in its most obvious meaning. It can provide sufficient knowledge for salvation without the expertise of any elite or special group or interpretive aid.

If we have the truth on the sanctuary doctrine, as we believe we do, then a scholarly look at all the evidence will add further force to the Seventh-day Adventist position. Thus what can be clear to the untrained mind is fully supported by the most careful work of the expert in languages or the skilled historian. What the average reader finds by comparing symbol with symbol, and Bible verse with Bible verse, the closest scrutiny of the most highly trained student of God's Word will also support.

We return briefly to the confusion introduced within the Seventh-day Adventist Church when A. F. Ballenger raised questions in 1905. As noted at the beginning, his teachings on the sanctuary as examined at the time of the General Conference session that year prompted Ellen White to suggest such a study as we have undertaken in this book. Regarding his erroneous teaching, she said:

> When the power of God testifies as to what is truth, that truth is to stand forever as the truth. No after suppositions contrary to the light God has given are to be entertained. Men will arise with interpretations of Scripture which are to them truth, but which are not truth. The truth for this time God has given us as a foundation for our faith. He Himself has taught us what is truth.—*Selected Messages*, book 1, p. 161 (see also letter 329, 1905).

She continued:

> We are not to receive the words of those who come with a message that contradicts the special points of our faith. They gather together a mass of Scripture, and pile it as proof around their asserted theories. This has been done over and over again during the past fifty years. And while the Scriptures are God's Word, and are to be respected, the application of them, if such application moves one pillar from the foundation that God has sustained these fifty years, is a great mistake. He who makes such an application knows not the wonderful demonstration of the Holy Spirit that gave power and force to the past messages that have come to the people of God.
>
> Elder G's* proofs are not reliable. If received, they would destroy the faith of God's people in the truth that has made us what we are.
>
> We must be decided on this subject; for the points that he is trying to prove by Scripture are not sound. They do not prove that the past experience of God's people was a fallacy. We had the truth; we were directed by the angels of God. It was under the guidance of the Holy

---

*The designation employed for Ballenger in *Selected Messages*, book 1.

Spirit that the presentation of the sanctuary question was given. It is eloquence for everyone to keep silent in regard to the features of our faith in which they acted no part. God never contradicts Himself. Scripture proofs are misapplied if forced to testify to that which is not true. Another and still another will arise and bring in supposedly great light, and make their assertions. But we stand by the old landmarks. [1 John 1:1-10 quoted.]—*Ibid.*, pp. 161, 162.

Referring to 1 John 1:1-10, Ellen White stated:

I am instructed to say that these words we may use as appropriate for this time, for the time has come when sin must be called by its right name. We are hindered in our work by men who are not converted, who seek their own glory. They wish to be thought originators of new theories, which they present claiming that they are truth. But if these theories are received, they will lead to a denial of the truth that for the past fifty years God has been giving to His people, substantiating it by the demonstration of the Holy Spirit.—*Ibid.*, p. 162.

Ballenger had a fatal flaw in his position. Rather than starting from the established Bible-based belief of the Adventist Church, he decided to take an independent beginning, choosing to ignore the careful study of the pioneers. It led him in a whole new direction, out of the Seventh-day Adventist Church, and to "private interpretation" of Scripture.

As with every doctrine Seventh-day Adventists believe, an understanding of the sanctuary and investigative judgment did not burst on our perception, correct in every detail, from the start. Intense study of Scripture and prayer for divine insight, mixed sometimes with tears, led our pioneers gradually to truth. Ellen White wrote:

The truths that have been unfolding in their order, as we have advanced along the line of prophecy revealed in the Word of God, are truth, sacred, eternal truth today. Those who passed over the ground step by step in the past history of our experience, seeing the chain of truth in the prophecies, were prepared to accept and obey every ray of light. They were praying, fasting, searching, digging for the truth as for hidden treasures, and the Holy Spirit, we know, was teaching and guiding us. Many theories were advanced, bearing a semblance of truth, but so mingled with misinterpreted and misapplied scriptures, that they led to dangerous errors.—*Selected Messages*, book 2, pp. 103, 104 (see also manuscript 31, 1896).

She continued:

The leadings of the Lord were marked, and most wonderful were

A CONCLUDING STATEMENT

His revelations of what is truth. Point after point was established by the Lord God of heaven. That which was truth *then*, is truth today. But the voices do not cease to be heard—"This is truth. I have new light." But these new lights in prophetic lines are manifest in misapplying the Word and setting the people of God adrift without an anchor to hold them.—*Ibid.*, p. 104.

At about the same time, Ellen White issued a caution as well as a challenge for us today:

Many will honestly search the Word for light as those in the past have searched it; and they see light in the Word. But they did not pass over the ground in their experience, when these messages of warning were first proclaimed. Not having had this experience, some do not appreciate the value of the truths that have been to us as waymarks, and that have made us as a peculiar people what we are.

They do not make a right application of the Scriptures, and thus they frame theories that are not correct. It is true that they quote an abundance of Scripture, and teach much that is true; but truth is so mixed with error as to lead to wrong conclusions. Yet because they can weave Scripture into their theories, they think they have a straight chain of truth. Many who did not have an experience in the rise of the messages, accept these erroneous theories, and are led into false paths, backward instead of forward. This is the enemy's design.—*Ibid.*, pp. 110, 111 (see also manuscript 32, 1896).

What a beautiful and comforting thought it is that Christ has our best interests at heart as He stands as our Advocate in heaven's sanctuary. Some have suggested that Christ is trying to see how many He can keep out of heaven. But it is not true. The work of investigation and judgment is His effort to see how many He can save. Writing in 1893, Ellen White urged:

Let us remember that our great High Priest is pleading before the mercy seat in behalf of His ransomed people. He ever liveth to make intercession for us. "If any man sin, we have an Advocate with the Father, Jesus Christ the righteous."

The blood of Jesus is pleading with power and efficacy for those who are backslidden, for those who are rebellious, for those who sin against great light and love. Satan stands at our right hand to accuse us, and our Advocate stands at God's right hand to plead for us. He has never lost a case that has been committed to Him.—*Seventh-day Adventist Bible Commentary*, vol. 7, p. 948 (see also RH, Aug. 15, 1893).

The teaching of the Seventh-day Adventist Church on the sanctuary and judgment is not hazy or uncertain. A remarkable fact is that Seventh-day Adventists clearly established their belief regarding the cleansing of the sanctuary by the time the church officially organized in 1863. General agreement on the doctrine has remained from that time to the present.

THE SANCTUARY, 1844, AND THE PIONEERS

Either Christ began the investigative judgment in 1844 or He did not. Either this church fulfills the prophecy regarding the remnant or it does not. Either we are preaching earth's last message of the three angels of Revelation 14 or we are not. Either the seventh-day Sabbath is God's seal on His people or it is not. Either Ellen White had the prophetic gift—and is God's special messenger—or she did not.

Voices within the Seventh-day Adventist Church today call for it to abandon historic and Bible-based belief regarding the sanctuary and its cleansing. Is the voice of the pioneers still worth listening to? Is their exposition of the prophecies trustworthy? We believe it is. And we believe an honest and careful study of the Bible evidences will bring us to the conclusion that they are right.

These last moments of our world's history are not a time to play intellectual games with the Scriptures. The positions of the pioneers came about through much prayer and Bible study. Then the visions given to Ellen G. White confirmed them. It is powerful evidence that we must not cast aside lightly.

But each person must make a decision for himself. Like the Bereans, who "searched the scriptures daily, whether those things were so" (Acts 17:11), we are to know and understand individually. The Seventh-day Adventist Church has preached longer than Noah did. His message was one to prepare for a flood, while ours is to prepare a dying world during a time of judgment for Christ's second coming. We believe it is the *last* message the world will receive before He returns. Thus we must know without question what we believe and why. The evidence from Scripture we must study for ourselves.

Surely it is not a time to begin new organizations or divide our message to the world. Satan would exult if such would happen. We are to give a clear, understandable proclamation that will draw people to Christ. He is the One who is about to finish His ministry in the Most Holy Place in heaven. When it is concluded, probation closes, and the final preparations begin for His triumphant return to earth as the King of the universe.

Our "adversary the devil, as a roaring lion, walketh about, seeking whom he may devour" (1 Peter 5:8). Will we let him detract us from preaching "the everlasting gospel" that tells the world that "the hour of his judgment is come" (Rev. 14:6, 7)? Each individual must answer that question. Sometimes the comments of the early pioneers had a certain "bite" to them. They spoke plainly as they met mockery or ridicule. They *had* to. Each believed that the

A CONCLUDING STATEMENT

Seventh-day Adventist Church had a clear message that would continue to the end of the reign of sin on earth. We must reaffirm that conviction personally today.

Comprehensive Periodical Listing

Articles in the *Review and Herald* and other Adventist Periodicals Regarding the Sanctuary, 1844, related events—1844-1905

WESTERN MIDNIGHT CRY

Enoch Jacobs
Nov. 29, 1844   Evidence That the Judgment Might Have Set on the Tenth Day of the Seventh Month
Dec. 30, 1844   Intolerance

THE ADVENT MIRROR

Apollos Hale, Joseph Turner
Jan., 1845

DAY-DAWN

O. R. L. Crosier
Winter, 1846   (No copy extant. Quoted in RH, May 5, 1851)

DAY-STAR

O. R. L. Crosier
Feb. 7, 1846   The Law of Moses

TRACTS, 1846-1850 (With Sanctuary Comments)

Joseph Bates
May, 1846   The Opening Heavens
Aug., 1846   The Seventh-day Sabbath, A Perpetual Sign
May, 1847   Second Advent Way Marks and High Heaps

COMPREHENSIVE PERIODICAL LISTING

| Jan., 1848 | A Vindication of the Seventh-day Sabbath and the Commandments of God |
| 1850 | An Explanation of the Typical and Anti-typical Sanctuary |

THE PRESENT TRUTH

Ellen G. White
Aug., 1849 — Dear Brethren and Sisters (Letter)
March, 1850 — My Dear Brethren and Sisters (Letter)

David Arnold
Dec., 1849 — The Shut Door Explained
March, 1850 — Daniel's Visions, the 2300 Days, and the Shut Door

James White
May, 1850 — The Sanctuary, 2300 Days, and the Shut Door

THE ADVENT REVIEW

O. R. L. Crosier
Sept., No. 3, 1850 — *Day-Star*, Feb. 7, 1846 (Excerpts)
Sept., No. 4, 1850 — *Day-Star*, Feb. 7, 1846 (Excerpts)

James White
Sept., No. 4, 1850 — The Day of Judgment

SECOND ADVENT REVIEW AND SABBATH HERALD

Joseph Bates
Nov., 1850 — The Laodicean Church
Dec., 1850 — Midnight Cry in the Past

Hiram Edson
March, 1851 — The Sixty-nine Weeks and 2300 Days

O. R. L. Crosier
May 5, 1851 — The Sanctuary (Reprint from *Day-Dawn*, 1845)
Sept. 2, 1852 — The Sanctuary (Reprint from *Day-Star*, Feb. 7, 1846)

James White
Dec., 1850 — Our Present Position
Jan., 1851 — Our Present Position
June 9, 1851 — The Parable, Matthew 25:1-12

THE ADVENT REVIEW AND SABBATH HERALD

James White
Feb. 17, 1852 — The Work of Grace

Feb. 17, 1852	Call at the Harbinger Office
May 27, 1852	The Ark and the Mercy-Seat
March 17, 1853	The Sanctuary and the 2300 Days
March 17, 1853	The Sanctuary
March 31, 1853	The Sanctuary
April 14, 1853	The Shut Door
April 28, 1853	Answers
Nov. 15, 1853	The Seventy Weeks
Dec. 6, 1853	The 2300 Days
April 4, 1854	The Seventy Weeks
April 18, 1854	The Twenty-three Hundred Days
Nov. 14, 1854	Exposition of Daniel 7
Nov. 21, 1854	Daniel, Chapters 8 and 9
Dec. 5, 1854	The Sanctuary
Jan. 29, 1857	The Judgment
Jan. 13, 1859	The Sanctuary
Jan. 20, 1859	The Sanctuary Again
June 24, 1862	Thoughts on the Revelation (Series)
July 1, 1862	"
Oct. 28, 1862	"
July 14, 1863	The Sanctuary (Series)
July 21, 1863	"
July 28, 1863	"
Aug. 4, 1863	"
Aug. 11, 1863	"
Aug. 18, 1863	"
Aug. 25, 1863	"
Sept. 1, 1863	"
Sept. 8, 1863	"
Dec. 1, 1863	The Sanctuary
May 5, 1868	*Life Incidents* (Excerpt)
Feb. 16, 1869	Saving Faith
Feb. 15, 1870	Our Faith and Hope (Series)
Feb. 22, 1870	"
March 1, 1870	"
March 8, 1870	"
March 15, 1870	"
March 22, 1870	"
April 5, 1870	"
April 19, 1870	"
April 26, 1870	"

J. N. Andrews

Dec. 23, 1852	The Sanctuary (Series)
Jan. 6, 1853	"
Jan. 20, 1853	"
Feb. 3, 1853	"
April 28, 1853	Answers
May 12, 1853	Position of the *Advent Herald* on the Sanctuary Question
May 12, 1853	The Cleansing of the Sanctuary
July 7, 1853	The Antitypical Tabernacle
Aug. 28, 1853	The Antitypical Tabernacle
Nov. 8, 1853	Under the Necessity of Choosing
Oct. 30, 1855	The Sanctuary and Its Cleansing
Feb. 21, 1856	The Cleansing of the Sanctuary
Oct. 18, 1864	The Sanctuary
April 6, 1869	The Opening of the Temple in Heaven
Nov. 9, 1869	The Order of Events in the Judgment (Series)
Nov. 16, 1869	"
Nov. 23, 1869	"
Nov. 30, 1869	"
Dec. 7, 1869	"
Dec. 14, 1869	"
Dec. 21, 1869	"
Dec. 28, 1869	"
Jan. 4, 1870	"
Jan. 11, 1870	"
Jan. 18, 1870	"
Jan. 25, 1870	"
Feb. 1, 1870	"
Feb. 8, 1870	"
Feb. 15, 1870	"
Feb. 22, 1870	"
March 1, 1870	"
March 8, 1870	"
March 15, 1870	"
March 22, 1870	"
Dec. 30, 1873	The Sanctuary of the Bible
March 10, 1874	The Sanctuary of the Bible
May 30, 1878	The Sanctuary

Uriah Smith

June 9, 1853	Letter
March 21, 1854	The Sanctuary (Series)

March 28, 1854	"
April 4, 1854	"
July 25, 1854	The Relation Which the Sabbath Sustains to Other Points of Present Truth
Jan. 9, 1855	The Sanctuary
Sept. 18, 1855	The Original Advent Faith
Oct. 2, 1855	The Cleansing of the Sanctuary
Nov. 27, 1856	The Scape-goat
Dec. 18, 1856	Is the Silence in Heaven During the Cleansing of the Sanctuary?
Jan. 29, 1857	The Hour of His Judgment Is Come
May 7, 1857	The 2300 Days. What Takes Place When They Terminate?
May 28, 1857	"And No Man Can Shut It"
Dec. 31, 1857	Synopsis of the Present Truth (Series)
Jan. 7, 1858	"
Jan. 14, 1858	"
Jan. 21, 1858	"
Jan. 28, 1858	"
Feb. 4, 1858	"
Feb. 11, 1858	"
Feb. 18, 1858	"
Feb. 25, 1858	"
March 11, 1858	"
March 18, 1858	"
March 25, 1858	"
April 1, 1858	"
April 8, 1858	"
April 15, 1858	"
April 22, 1858	"
April 29, 1858	"
May 20, 1858	"
June 10, 1858	"
May 29, 1860	The 2300 Days
Nov. 1, 1864	The Sanctuary—An Objection Considered
Dec. 6, 1864	Hard Pressed for Dates
June 12, 1866	The 2300 Days
June 25, 1867	A Work of Judgment
June 8, 1869	Thoughts on the Book of Daniel (Series)
June 15, 1869	"
June 21, 1870	"
June 28, 1870	"

July 5, 1870	"
July 12, 1870	"
July 19, 1870	"
July 26, 1870	"
Aug. 2, 1870	"
Aug. 9, 1870	"
Aug. 16, 1870	"
Aug. 23, 1870	"
Aug. 30, 1870	"
Sept. 6, 1870	"
Sept. 13, 1870	"
Sept. 20, 1870	"
Oct. 4, 1870	"
April 8, 1873	The Vail of the Sanctuary
Jan. 6, 1874	The Hour of His Judgment Come (Series)
Jan. 13, 1874	The Judgment of Revelation 14:7
Jan. 20, 1874	Time of the Judgment of Revelation 14:7
Dec. 22, 1874	The Sanctuary
July 29, 1875	Questions on the Sanctuary
Aug. 5, 1875	"
Jan. 6, 1876	The Sanctuary (Series)
Jan. 13, 1876	"
Jan. 20, 1876	"
Jan. 27, 1876	"
Feb. 3, 1876	"
Feb. 10, 1876	"
Feb. 17, 1876	"
Feb. 24, 1876	"
March 2, 1876	"
March 9, 1876	"
March 16, 1876	"
March 23, 1876	"
March 30, 1876	"
April 6, 1876	"
April 13, 1876	"
April 20, 1876	"
April 27, 1876	"
May 4, 1876	"
May 11, 1876	"
May 18, 1876	"
May 25, 1876	"
June 1, 1876	"

June 8, 1876	"
June 15, 1876	"
June 22, 1876	"
June 29, 1876	"
July 6, 1876	"
July 13, 1876	"
July 20, 1876	"
July 27, 1876	"
Aug. 3, 1876	"
Aug. 10, 1876	"
Aug. 17, 1876	"
Aug. 24, 1876	"
Aug. 31, 1876	"
Oct. 19, 1876	"
Oct. 26, 1876	"
Nov. 2, 1876	"
Nov. 9, 1876	"
Nov. 16, 1876	"
Nov. 23, 1876	"
Nov. 30, 1876	"
Dec. 7, 1876	"
Nov. 22, 1881	The Great Central Subject
Feb. 20, 1883	The Sanctuary
June 5, 1883	The Sanctuary
June 12, 1883	A Work of Judgment
July 3, 1883	Satan as the Scape-goat
Oct. 16, 1883	Miller's Mistake
Feb. 5, 1884	Questions on the Sanctuary
Dec. 16, 1884	The Atonement (Book Review)
Jan. 6, 1885	The Parable of the Ten Virgins
Jan. 13, 1885	"
Feb. 3, 1885	The Judgment of the Great Day (Series)
Feb. 10, 1885	"
Feb. 17, 1885	"
Feb. 24, 1885	"
March 3, 1885	"
March 10, 1885	"
March 17, 1885	"
March 24, 1885	"
March 31, 1885	"
April 7, 1885	"
April 14, 1885	"

April 21, 1885	"
April 28, 1885	"
May 5, 1885	"
Jan. 5, 1886	The Angel's Answer
March 23, 1886	The Judgment Now Passing
June 29, 1886	The Sanctuary
March 1, 1887	The Marriage of the Lamb
June 14, 1887	Questions on the Sanctuary
June 28, 1887	The Sanctuary
Aug. 2, 1887	J. W. Morton and the Sanctuary Question
Sept. 27, 1887	The Sanctuary
March 6, 1888	Between the Cherubim
March 13, 1888	Then Shall the Sanctuary Be Cleansed
April 17, 1888	Not the Very Image
April 24, 1888	Was Christ a Priest on Earth?
May 1, 1888	The Blood of Christ
May 8, 1888	The Chronological Position of the Atonement
May 15, 1888	The Final Separation
May 22, 1888	The Investigative Judgment
Dec. 17, 1889	History and Prophecy
Jan. 14, 1890	The Vail of Hebrews 6
Jan. 21, 1890	Queries on the Sanctuary
Feb. 4, 1890	The Coming of the Lord
Feb. 11, 1890	"
March 4, 1890	The Covenant of Hebrews 9:1
Dec. 16, 1890	Origin and History of Third Angel's Message (Series)
Jan. 6, 1891	"
Jan. 13, 1891	"
June 16, 1891	The Days of the Seventh Angel
July 14, 1891	S.D. Adventists and the Atonement
March 21, 1893	To Make Intercession
June 20, 1893	Thou Shalt Stand in Thy Lot
Oct. 3, 1893	The Heavenly Things
Oct. 10, 1893	From Old to New
Oct. 17, 1893	The Cleansing of the Sanctuary
Oct. 24, 1893	Christ the Perfect Priest
Oct. 31, 1893	The Living Way
Jan. 30, 1894	The Atonement
May 15, 1894	The Angel's Answer
Jan. 1, 1895	The Sanctuary
Nov. 12, 1895	The Mystery of God

THE SANCTUARY, 1844, AND THE PIONEERS

OTHER AUTHORS

The following articles appear chronologically except for extended series by some authors.

COMPREHENSIVE PERIODICAL LISTING

C. W. Sperry

    Feb. 7, 1856   The Sanctuary

E. Everts

    June 11, 1857   A Few Thoughts on the Cleansing of the Sanctuary

Hiram Edson

    July 30, 1857   Daniel Standing in His Lot

J. N. Loughborough

    Nov. 19, 1857   The Judgment
    Jan. 27, 1859   Bible Class at Portland, Maine

J. H. Waggoner

    Oct. 6, 1863   The Atonement (Series)
    Nov. 17, 1863   "
    Nov. 24, 1863   "
    Dec. 1, 1863   "
    Aug. 23, 1864   "
    Aug. 30, 1864   "
    Sept. 6, 1864   "

Roswell F. Cottrell

    Dec. 15, 1863   The Sanctuary
    Sept. 20, 1864   Sanctuary and Synagogues

J. N. Loughborough

    Aug. 15, 1865   Thoughts on the Day of Atonement

Charles Beecher

    March 13, 1866   Azazel or Satan

George C. Cochran

    Dec. 18, 1866   The 2300 Days

Roswell F. Cottrell

    March 26, 1867   The Time Message

A. C. Bourdeau

    May 14, 1867   Our Present Position
    May 28, 1867   "

D. M. Canright

    Jan. 19, 1869   The Two Absurdities

THE SANCTUARY, 1844, AND THE PIONEERS

W. H. Blaisdell

Feb. 16, 1869   Sinners May Yet Obtain Mercy

D. M. Canright

May 11, 1869   The Different Offices and Positions of Jesus Christ

May 18, 1869   The Judgment Is Past Before the Lord Comes

J. N. Loughborough

Aug. 24, 1869   The Judgment

Roswell F. Cottrell

Sept. 28, 1869   The Closing Messages

J. H. Waggoner

June 21, 1870   Review of Wellcome and Goud (Introduction only)

July 5, 1870   "

Roswell F. Cottrell

Oct. 11, 1870   A.D. 1844

J. H. Waggoner

May 19, 1874   *The Atonement* (Series [Revision of 1863-1864 Series])

May 26, 1874   "
June 2, 1874   "
June 16, 1874   "
June 23, 1874   "
June 30, 1874   "
July 7, 1874   "

Roswell F. Cottrell

Nov. 17, 1874   Light From the Sanctuary

J. G. Matteson

Nov. 23, 1876   The Priesthood of the New Testament

Goodloe Harper Bell

Oct. 31, 1878   Lessons for Bible Classes
Nov. 14, 1878   "
Nov. 21, 1878   "
Nov. 28, 1878   "

Dec. 5, 1878   "
Dec. 12, 1878   "
Dec. 19, 1878   "

D. T. Bourdeau

Nov. 27, 1879   Refutation of the Doctrine of Instantaneous Sanctification

W. H. Littlejohn

Nov. 27, 1879   The Cleansing of the Sanctuary, and the Judgment

J. O. Corliss

Feb. 26, 1880   The 2300 Days

Joseph Clarke

June 17, 1880   The Sanctuary

F. Peabody

Dec. 9, 1880   The Tarrying Lord

Mrs. M. E. Steward

Oct. 18, 1881   The Day of Atonement

H. Wren

Dec. 12, 1882   The Cleansing of the Sanctuary

H. A. St. John

Feb. 13, 1883   Synopsis of the Atonement
Feb. 20, 1883   "

Roswell F. Cottrell

April 17, 1883   The Ark of the Testimony
March 11, 1884   The Cleansing of the Sanctuary (Series)
March 18, 1884   "
March 25, 1884   "
April 1, 1884   "
April 8, 1884   "
April 15, 1884   "
April 22, 1884   "
April 29, 1884   "

J. P. Henderson

April 8, 1884   Books in Heaven

THE SANCTUARY, 1844, AND THE PIONEERS

W. H. Littlejohn

July 22, 1884	The Temple in Heaven (Series)
July 29, 1884	"
Aug. 5, 1884	"
Aug. 12, 1884	"
Aug. 19, 1884	"
Aug. 26, 1884	"
Sept. 2, 1884	"
Sept. 9, 1884	"
Sept. 16, 1884	"
Sept. 23, 1884	"
Oct. 7, 1884	"
Oct. 13, 1884	"
Oct. 20, 1884	"
Oct. 27, 1884	"
Nov. 4, 1884	"
Nov. 11, 1884	"
Nov. 18, 1884	"

D. M. Canright

Dec. 23, 1884	Our Mediator

N. J. Bowers

Jan. 20, 1885	The Margin of Daniel 8:14

G. B. Thompson

Sept. 15, 1885	A Solemn Thought

J. G. Mattison

April 26, 1887	The Investigative Judgment
May 24, 1887	The Visions of Daniel and John

Washington Morse

Sept. 25, 1888	Items of Advent Experience

Sabbath School Lesson Notes

April 2, 1889
April 9, 1889

Bible Reading on the Sanctuary

July 23, 1889
July 30, 1889
Aug. 6, 1889
Aug. 27, 1889

COMPREHENSIVE PERIODICAL LISTING

Sabbath School Lesson Notes

    Dec. 24, 1889
    Jan. 14, 1890
    Jan. 21, 1890

R. A. Underwood

    Sept. 21, 1889   Christ and His Work

D. T. Bourdeau

    Oct. 29, 1889   The Value of Prophetic Periods in Study of Prophecy

    Nov. 5, 1889   "

Roswell F. Cottrell

    Feb. 11, 1890   Names Written in Heaven

L. A. Smith

    March 4, 1890   Sin and the Atonement

N. Paquette

    June 3, 1890   The Judgment

W. H. Littlejohn

    Oct. 20, 1891   The Judgment and the Papacy

L. A. Smith

    April 19, 1892   The Supreme Court

Bible Study

    Nov. 14, 1893   Sanctuary

Joseph Clarke

    April 3, 1894   The Judgment

G. C. Tenney

    Jan. 1, 1895   Lessons on the Sanctuary—Sabbath School
    Jan. 8, 1895   "
    Jan. 22, 1895   "
    Jan. 29, 1895   "
    Feb. 5, 1895   "

W. W. Prescott

    Feb. 5, 1895   The Sanctuary and Its Services (Series)
    Feb. 12, 1895   "

THE SANCTUARY, 1844, AND THE PIONEERS

Feb. 19, 1895   "

J. E. Evans

March 24, 1896   When Did Christ Become Priest?

W. W. Prescott

Aug. 31, 1897   The Hour of His Judgment (Series)
Sept. 7, 1897   "

G. E. Fifield

Sept. 21, 1897   Cleansing of the Sanctuary

Washington Morse

Nov. 23, 1897   A Letter
March 7, 1899   The Cleansing of the Sanctuary

Luther Burgess

June 12, 1900   The Hour of God's Judgment Is Come

S. N. Haskell

Sept. 4, 1900   Importance of an Understanding of Christ's
                    Work in the Heavenly Sanctuary
Aug. 13, 1901   The Sanctuary Question From the Standpoint
                    of the Book of Hebrews (Series)
Aug. 20, 1901   "
Aug. 27, 1901   "

G. B. Thompson

Oct. 8, 1901   A Solemn Fact

B. L. Howe

Dec. 10, 1901   The Judgment

Washington Morse

Oct. 28, 1902   Early and Late Experiences

Mrs. S. N. Haskell

Feb. 18, 1904   The Sanctuary (Series)
Feb. 25, 1904   "
March 3, 1904   "

S. N. Haskell

Oct. 27, 1904   The Sanctuary (Series)
Nov. 3, 1904   "

Nov. 10, 1904   "
Nov. 17, 1904   "
Dec. 1, 1904   "
Dec. 15, 1904   "
Dec. 22, 1904   "
Dec. 29, 1904   "

W. W. Prescott

Feb. 9, 1905   A Personal Saviour and a Real Work in a Definite Place